More praise for Positively Confidential

"The capacity to transform information into intellectual assets is realized only if the process is easy and the rewards are substantial. *Positively Confidential* is a catalyst for both. An essential read for everyone in the workforce."

Shash Patel, *Director, Information Risk Management & Privacy, Air Products and Chemicals, Inc.*

"Finally, a book about protecting intangible assets with a much-needed message: confidentiality is positive. This book reveals, in detail, how great organizations build and maintain a culture that respects and protects the value of their information. Don't just read it; use it to make a difference in your organization!"

John Tanner, *Information Protection Officer, Boehringer Ingelheim USA*

"With *Positively Confidential*, Naomi Fine builds on her decades of experience in managing corporate confidentiality. She squarely confronts one of the most critical issues facing today's globalized businesses and, in the process, delivers a prescription that is comprehensive, easy to read, and full of practical solutions."

James Pooley, *Deputy Director General for Innovation and Technology, World Intellectual Property Organization, author of the treatise Trade Secrets, Former Adjunct Professor teaching about trade secrets, Boalt Hall Law School, University of California at Berkeley*

"*Positively Confidential* belongs on the desk of every corporate citizen. Naomi Fine ... demystifies a subject of complex proportions and brings it into easy focus. Clear, concise, comprehensive, and accessible, *Positively Confidential* will be seen as a seminal work on information protection."

Ilene E. Coon, *Senior Director, Global Security Programs and Strategic Planning, Seagate Technology*

D0943062

Positively Confidential

Positively Confidential

10 Proven Steps to Protecting
Confidential Information, Private Data,
and Intellectual Property in
Today's Interactive Business World

Naomi Fine, Esq.

Library of Congress Control Number: 2010918433

ISBN: 978-0-9800268-0-1

Published by Reasonable Measures Publishing, Los Altos, CA 94022
In cooperation with Pro-Tec Data, Los Altos, CA 94022

Cover design, graphics and text layout design by: MCD Advertising & Design, Manhattan Beach, CA 90266

Author's photograph by Maddy Klein, Weinberg-Clark Photography, Mountain View, CA 94043

Printed in the United States of America

Contents

Tables

Figures

*To your innovative potential
and its use as a powerful force for good.*

Acknowledgments

This book is only possible because of the hundreds of chief executive officers, general counsels, chief information security officers, chief privacy officers, senior corporate security officers, as well as many others whose job it is to protect their organization's intellectual assets, who entrusted me as a strategic partner. Their stories, experiences, knowledge, and framings, as well as their trust and confidence in me to help them solve problems, created an essential foundation for my know-how. I am eternally grateful to the leaders who have allowed me to collaborate with them over the years to meet their challenges to safeguard information and intellectual property. I thank every Pro-Tec Data client for giving me the opportunity to build and strengthen my expertise and to see firsthand how their organizations need an employee-friendly reference book to explain why corporate citizens should—and easily can—protect confidential information.

I also thank Susan Thomas, an accomplished business strategist, communicator, and writer, who coached me through creating a vision and outline for this book. Susan's guidance and her detailed conceptual feedback to my early manuscript transformed my book ideas into something concrete and viable.

My sister Terri Susan Fine, a political science professor at the University of Central Florida and an extraordinary technical editor, was patient and responsive in editing the initial book manuscript.

My sister Debra Fine, keynote speaker, trainer, and bestselling author of *The Fine Art of Small Talk: How to Start a Conversation, Keep it Going, Build Rapport and Leave a Positive Impression* and *The Fine Art of the Big Talk: How to Win Clients, Deliver Great Presentations, and Solve Conflicts at Work*, was my inspiration, advisor, and role model.

I owe a debt of gratitude to David Davis of MCD Advertising & Design for his creativity and responsiveness in designing the book, including its cover, graphics, and style guide. Sarah Granger provided editorial assistance, for which I am grateful. I also thank Russell Cameron Thomas, who helped shape the introduction.

I thank Yvonne Kisiel, Dave Torrey, David Best, Alexis Tatarsky, and Cynthia Schultz for their interest and feedback. I thank Shelley Lapkoff and Jeremy Sherman for being loyal friends and listening as I discussed the book's progress over many years.

I am especially grateful to my family who constantly show me how love and wisdom are expressed in infinite ways. Kathy Levinson, my hero, provided editorial guidance as well as her gentle encouragement and moral support, without which this book may never have been completed. Parker and Reade gave me great ideas as well as their unwavering confidence in my ability to succeed.

I am also grateful to my parents, who gave me the gift of life and the intelligence and chutzpah to make the most of it.

Foreword

Protecting information is no longer an option in the modern corporate and regulatory environment. It's a business fundamental. As I learned while developing an information security program at Levi's, Safeway, and Hewlett-Packard, today's valued customers are often tomorrow's formidable competitors.

I've spent much of my career focusing on protecting critical business information in large enterprises. This complex area requires an interdisciplinary approach with the involvement of information technology (IT) security, legal, compliance, corporate security, risk management, audit, human resources, employee communication specialists, and others. A successful program must fit the corporate culture and be easily recognized as relevant by all employees.

Although it's critical for enterprises to protect information, it has always been difficult to involve employees because they often view it as complex, too time-consuming, or someone else's responsibility. A comprehensive strategy requires a significant investment in resources and a commitment to a long-term solution that must evolve over time in an environment of constant, rapid change. Vital to any strategy is the active involvement of all stakeholders who have access to a company's valuable information. Without their strong, visible support, no amount of technical security or law and policy enforcement will succeed.

In this book, Naomi Fine has nailed the keys to success and return on investment. *Positively Confidential* makes available to every employee, contractor, supplier, and customer a simple, compelling guide to being a more effective soldier in the battle for achieving corporate objectives and protecting competitive advantage. When I first engaged Naomi's services to develop a trading partner security program at Levi's, I felt I had struck gold in finding her. She is a thought leader who excels at distilling the key elements of information protection into easily understood, relevant concepts. *Positively Confidential* delivers many nuggets of wisdom to inspire all stakeholders to protect the lifeblood of their company.

Sherry Ryan,
former Chief Information Security Officer,
Hewlett-Packard Company

Introduction

A vision care company led in best-of-breed equipment development, but they received no competitive advantage from it. They wanted their market position to match their innovation leadership and sought my help. In this company, a team of engineers was responsible for designing equipment used to manufacture contact lenses. The engineers openly discussed their challenges and potential solutions with equipment vendors and industry colleagues because their exclusive goal was to develop durable, low-maintenance equipment that consistently produced high-quality products using minimal resources. The information the engineers shared was widely disseminated in technical papers and conference presentations. Ultimately, the vision care company's competitors used it to improve their own products.

My goal after evaluating the situation was to help the engineers see their jobs differently. I explained that they could optimize their value within the company if their work focused on creating the *intellectual property* (intangible assets such as patents and trade secrets) for durable, low-maintenance equipment that consistently produced high-quality products using minimal resources. If they only focused on developing the equipment while allowing competitors to develop similar equipment, both the engineers' and the equipment's value to the company would be short-lived. If they developed intellectual property, such as manufacturing process trade secrets and equipment part patents, their value to the company and the value of their company's intellectual property were considerably higher.

Once the engineers changed their perspectives and started protecting their ideas as intellectual property, rather than sharing product and process information freely, the company was able to preclude competitors from developing, using, and selling the same equipment. Charging license fees to other companies for their right to use the know-how and inventions developed by the vision care company engineers also became an option for my client. As a result of their new approach, the company's profits skyrocketed.

The engineers made impactful changes in a short period by identifying and protecting their company's confidential information using the ten steps I describe in this book. In helping their company, they also helped themselves, as each engineer received a substantial raise to reflect the increased profits that the employer garnered. Several of these engineers confided to me that they felt tremendous satisfaction knowing that their work was now contributing significantly to their company's stronger competitive advantage, enhanced profitability, and increased growth of their company. The vision care company's transformation is just one of many examples that illustrate how individuals and companies can reap rewards from sharing *and protecting* ideas and information.

In my experience working with diverse organizations, corporate citizens contribute more to their company's success and avoid the trouble that results from acting inconsistently with their company's best interests by putting greater attention on safeguarding confidential information. You likely have access to confidential information that may come from your company, its business partners, customers, suppliers, contractors, or other stakeholders. If so, your job includes protecting information whether you are a line worker, manager, or executive. Confidential information may be owned by

- Your company (subject to policy requirements)
- Another company (subject to contractual obligations)
- Individuals (subject to privacy laws)

Being trusted with that information and knowing when, how, and with whom to share it is key to your own and your company's advancement. Lax information safeguards erode trust, an essential characteristic of every individual and corporate player in today's business environment.

At the same time, it is becoming easier every year to leak corporate secrets quickly and on a massive scale. Computers and communication devices are now ubiquitous, mobile, and networked together in a variety of ways. Information can be transmitted or copied easily, quickly, and wirelessly (and without a trace in many cases), making it harder to control and easier to lose or exploit. Threats continue to escalate as we move from the Information Age to the Web 2.0 and Web 3.0 Age. It is more likely than ever that someone somewhere will try to take advantage of valuable information without paying a price.

Corporate survival is at stake. Millions of dollars worth of ideas, information, designs, formulas, and relationships can be lost or stolen with the click of a mouse. More regulations and litigation mean that the risks, including the monetary and reputational costs of threatened and actual litigation and legal liability, are increasing. Changing corporate structures, employee turnover, outsourcing, and globalization all multiply the complexities that open information to danger.

Still, protecting information does not require absolute secrecy. Rather, it is a high stakes balancing act between openness and security. Openness can enhance productivity, efficiency, and global reach. People and companies now connect using a new breed of information-sharing and collaboration technologies, including groupware, wikis, blogs, and social networking. It is becoming standard practice for companies to use these interactive business communications tools to produce, market, and sell products; obtain positive media coverage; recruit investors; and conduct day-to-day business. Protecting certain information from (and, in some cases, within) this interactive process enables a company to differentiate itself in the marketplace, establish legal rights, sustain competitive advantages, control media messaging, maintain customer and shareholder trust, and avoid claims of misappropriation. In an environment where the forces of openness and security coexist, it is more crucial than ever to know what is to be held confidential and how to create the right conditions for safe information exchange. If you don't know what you are doing, you can cause a lot of damage with no ill intentions and little effort.

Consider the sales representative who is responsible for enticing prospective customers on his company's merits without revealing his company's unreleased, next-generation product offering. He may tell the prospect that his company has some "new and exciting improvements soon to be released that will address even more of his customer's needs" without divulging any specific details. If someone in his company shares particulars about the new product on a blog and the prospect finds it while searching the Web, the prospect could put together enough information to discover the new product's features. As a result, the sales rep and his company would lose credibility with the prospect for claiming that the information was confidential. If the prospect shares the information with the rep's competitor to get a bid and the competitor uses the information to improve its own product or accelerate a new product announcement, the rep's company may forfeit its market timing and first mover advantage. When secrecy is removed, its value and competitive advantages are lost. The company loses the benefit of a controlled new product launch, and the sales rep tarnishes his relationship with the prospect because the information the rep claimed to be confidential can be learned through other means.

Rumors of new products and product specification documents are leaked almost every day through the blogosphere. With the tools presented in this book, every employee and entrepreneur can be part of a corporate culture that minimizes these leaks and their unwanted and unintended consequences.

That is why it is *every* employee's job to protect information, no matter what else her position entails. Anyone with access to a company's confidential information must actively protect it. Otherwise, there may be no company of value left to protect.

Employee and company pursuits are each best served by a cautious blend of revealing and safeguarding information. In the case of the vision care company, for example, the engineers were not forced into complete silence and away from information exchange. Protecting information does not mean ironclad security. Rather, the objective is to strike the right balance between the compelling business needs to share information and the competing business and legal interests in protecting it. *Positively Confidential* will help you to both share and protect sensitive company information to benefit you and your company. Anyone with access to nonpublic company information can become a more valuable and trusted stakeholder by applying the ten proven steps this book describes.

The vision care company engineers learned the power of revealing information intentionally, consciously, and in a manner that targeted specific outcomes. They also learned the control and power of holding back, restricting access, limiting authorized use of revealed secrets, and ensuring that anyone entrusted with valuable information safeguards its value. Applying the positively confidential approach, the engineers balanced the tension between their desires to share information and the equally crucial need to protect it. The engineers disclosed information to advisors, contractors, and suppliers, but only under circumstances that ensured that the information would be used for their company's benefit. They created an ecosystem in which all those with access to their confidential information safeguarded it, making the vision care company more secure for information sharing.

The vision care company is not alone in making this highly profitable transformation. As founder and CEO of Pro-Tec Data for more than twenty-five years, I have helped hundreds of world-class companies profit from addressing their information protection challenges including

Apple Computer	International Paper	Rockwell International
Applied Materials	Johnson & Johnson	Ralston Purina
Baxter Healthcare	Levi Strauss	SC Johnson Wax
Bristol-Myers Squibb	McDonald's	Safeway
Cablevision	Michelin	Seagate Technology
Caterpillar	Nestle	Sun Microsystems
Charles Schwab	Nortel Networks	Symantec
Deloitte, Touch & Tohmatsu	Philip Morris	TD Ameritrade
Eastman Kodak	Procter & Gamble	Visa
Intel Corporation	Qualcomm	Xerox

These companies from diverse industries ask me questions such as

- What should we consider confidential?
- How should we protect it?
- What are the best information protection practices in a globalized, outsourced enterprise?
- How do we comply with laws, regulations, and other expectations that our business partners, customers, and government entities impose on us?
- How do we effectively protect the information we need to share with our on- and offshore partners?

Yet the most pressing and prevalent question of all is, "How should we help our employees, contractors, and other stakeholders with access to our information understand the importance of protecting it and make doing so easy and integral to their everyday jobs?" This question likely prompted you to read this book or prompted a co-worker or your boss to want you to read it. The question has become even more urgent with the evolution of Web 2.0 and Web 3.0 technologies, where interactive information-sharing opportunities are abundant and replete with momentous benefits and risks.

It is in every stakeholder's interest to become part of an active ecosystem that, with good intentions and only a little effort, can make a big difference. The challenge for you and your company is to make protecting information an easy and integral part of what you do, not an annoyance or distraction from your primary work. Protecting information may feel inconvenient if you don't understand its importance. You already have plenty to do. The last thing you need is an administrative hassle to distract you from getting your primary work done. Even if you already understand how urgent protecting information is to your own and your company's success, you still might hesitate to do what is required if it feels complicated, burdensome, or extraneous to your other job responsibilities.

I wrote this book not only to help you see the benefits of protecting your company's confidential information, but to make it simple even as you take advantage of new interactive business opportunities like social media outreach. *Positively Confidential* presents the essential elements of your responsibilities to protect information synthesized in ten steps that are easy to apply while accomplishing your main job:

1. Know why protecting information matters.
2. Understand the risks of not protecting information.
3. Identify the information you need to protect.
4. Make it clear that confidential information is indeed confidential.
5. Determine your need to reveal before you share confidential information.
6. Limit confidential information exposure.
7. Apply digital security basics.
8. Construct the appropriate precautionary force field.

9. Fulfill confidentiality obligations to others.

10. Support your company's information protection ecosystem.

Each of the ten steps is explained in a separate chapter, structured to highlight the core points, and reinforced with takeaways and a spot quiz that underscore its essential elements. The afterword compiles all ten steps and takeaways. You can find an answer key to the spot quizzes in appendix D.

The ten steps do not cover every possible action item, which could number in the hundreds. Using the 90/10 rule, however, you will achieve at least 90 percent of the positively confidential outcomes with these ten steps. By applying them consistently, you will make smart decisions about sharing information as you engage with business associates, use social media, transmit information with the latest digital gadgets and online services, or encounter scams. You will position yourself and your company to make confidential information available strategically and safely. You will also minimize the likelihood of causing or being an accomplice to a confidentiality breach. By adopting these ten steps to protect information, you will help your company capitalize on its intellectual property and create new revenue streams. Protecting information *and* sharing it under the right circumstances will keep you out of trouble, establish trusting relationships between you and those with whom you work, and increase your company's profitability and growth. Consequently, you will likely reap rewards and enhance your career prospects.

The vision care company engineers were able to alter their corporate landscape in positive ways to raise morale, recognize the engineers' good ideas, nurture innovation, increase profits, and earn better salaries. Like the vision care company engineers, you can transform information into valuable secrets. Your firm can take advantage of its new upside opportunities that grow from creating profit-generating intellectual assets. Making good decisions about when, with whom, and how to share information will also help you avoid the devastation and humiliation of being careless with confidential information.

As an information protection expert, I encourage all business leaders, entrepreneurs, and employees of every talent and function to embrace the interesting and necessary challenges of safeguarding information, particularly in the face of interactive media and enabling technologies. Your information protection efforts foster a nurturing atmosphere for innovation and collaboration. You amplify this effort's value to you and your company by leading fellow employees, contractors, consultants, supply chain partners, and other stakeholders to join you in creating a positively confidential ecosystem.

Know Why
Protecting Information Matters

CHAPTER 1

Chapter 1 Takeaways

Why does protecting information matter?

- Keeping information confidential creates value that allows you and your company to reap your work's rewards.

- Your information protection efforts are essential to achieving your organization's strategic objectives.

- Unprotected information can cause very messy and expensive losses.

Two Truths about Protecting Information

After more than twenty-five years of helping hundreds of companies from diverse industries and working directly with corporate citizens at every level, from boards of directors and CEOs to administrative assistants and line workers, I know that only two truths will motivate you to protect information:

- If you do, you will gain more than the effort you put in.
- If you do not, you will lose much more than it takes to avoid the loss.

Information is a company's essence. It distinguishes an organization and makes it unique in its market. What you do with information determines if your company is a winner or a loser. Broadcasting promotional literature can build a brand and gain market share while publicizing product development processes can cause company failure.

Understanding what should be kept confidential and protecting that information makes you an important contributor to your company's strong and distinctive worth. It also makes your company a more valued trading partner. Inadequate information protection and the resulting lost competitiveness, tarnished reputation, liability, and distraction diminishes your contribution and is an impediment to others trusting your company or appreciating its value.

Today's collaborative, digital, and interactive business environment propels openness, sharing, and information exchange. Protecting confidential information complements these activities by enabling their rewards and avoiding their potential hazards.

What Is Positively Confidential?

Positively confidential is an approach to business interactions that creates a safe haven for developing, holding, and sharing any information that has special value in an organization, including sensitive data, unique know-how, and trade secrets. Such havens fuel lucrative relationships with people and ideas. You, your fellow employees, and other company stakeholders build positively confidential containers to protect confidential information, intellectual property, and customer privacy.

As commerce expands from collaborating, connecting, and becoming more interactive, every company needs a positively confidential ecosystem where partners and customers feel safe revealing their confidential and private information. Even open source (peer development with open access to the end product's source materials), crowd-sourced (development by open call to a community), networked innovation (development by an external network of individual experts, academics, and organizations), and other open collaboration communities thrive from the freedom to participate that emerges from a clear understanding of who owns what information and intellectual property before and after development. Precautions support sharing and encourage information cross-fertilization. When companies and their business partners have confidence in their employees' ability to protect confidential information, they are more likely to be open about communicating information that will drive further customer trust and collaboration and increase market share. Co-creating a positively confidential atmosphere with your work colleagues boosts your company's opportunities to achieve marketplace success while improving your own ability to advance in your profession as you become a more meaningful contributor to your company's accomplishments.

Helping Achieve Your Organization's Strategic Objectives

Protecting confidential information, including customers' private data, helps achieve your organization's strategic objectives because it supports your company's growth, profitability, and innovation leadership. While disseminating information also plays a major role in these achievements, thoughtfully executed openness entails a foundation of information controls.

The senior executives of my Fortune 500 clients frequently ask me to help them implement information protection strategies to reach their corporate aspirations. The proactive initiatives that build positively confidential working environments have proven significantly beneficial for their own and their company's fortunes.

The following table lists the strategic objectives common to many of my Fortune 500 clients and summarizes the information protection outcomes that support each of these objectives.

How Information Protection Supports Strategic Business Objectives	
Strategic Business Objective	**Information Protection Outcomes**
Differentiation and Industry Leadership	– Creates the mystery and proprietary rights that make a company unique in its markets
Growth	– Ensures ownership of intellectual assets – Enables customer and business partner relationship expansion – Reduces the high cost of information loss, damage control, business relationship failures, and litigation
High Performance Work Environment ("Great Place to Work")	– Motivates the best and brightest to discover and develop intellectual property, enhancing the employment proposition for everyone developing it because individual value is recognized and rewarded
Product/Service and Operational Excellence	– Contributes to product/service development and operational excellence by protecting the quality and integrity of decisions based on company information
Efficiency	– Improves the company's time to market by avoiding the cost and distraction of unwanted disclosures
Marketing Punch	– Allows each product launch and promotional campaign to be met with surprise – Controls the timing of announcements and messaging

Prestige and Reputation	— Builds the perception that the company has value, strength, mystery, and competence — Minimizes the risk of tarnishing reputations because of inappropriate information disclosure
Customer Intimacy	— Builds customer confidence that the company's intellectual resources are strong and the company is capable of protecting information entrusted to it — Makes the company more trustworthy and reduces risks associated with partnerships
Trust	— Establishes responsibilities for safeguarding information, enabling safe openness and collaboration

Table 1

Discovering the correlation between protecting information and meeting business objectives helps employees at every organizational level to support their organization's ability to be an establishment where they are proud to work. The more effective you become at fulfilling the responsibilities associated with receiving and revealing confidential information, the more you contribute to your company's high-performance culture based on excellence and a great reputation.

If you embrace a positively confidential approach to protecting information about the big project you just finished, your company can own the resulting ideas, plans, designs, and inventions. Occasionally, you may want to keep the new project secret by operating in stealth mode and sharing no information about it. More often, you will need to protect information by striking the right balance between competing interests in revealing and concealing information. If that new project would benefit from having an outside expert assist with research or development, it may be helpful to divulge sensitive research planning information to the outsider. The key to a positively confidential approach is to understand what information you should disclose to the expert and how to do so with mechanisms that reduce the likelihood that she will use the information contrary to your company's best interests. I discuss these tactics in subsequent chapters.

Your discretion is equally important to an organization-wide, positively confidential effort. What you and your colleagues do, individually and cooperatively, matters. If everyone works together to protect company confidential information, you convert it into legally recognized assets, which power business success.

Trade Secret Rights

Trade secrets are legally recognized and potent intangible assets. Most states in the United States and the federal government will recognize the following as a trade secret:

- Any information, including a formula, pattern, compilation, program, device, method, technique, or process;
- That derives independent economic value, actual or potential, from not being generally known to or ascertainable by others;
- If it is treated with measures that can reasonably be expected to preserve its secrecy (Section 1 (4) of the Uniform Trade Secrets Act, 1990).

You help confer legal ownership and property rights to information by protecting it. You create intellectual property—specifically, the legal ownership rights of trade secrets—by applying reasonable measures to protect valuable information that is not available to the public. A key ingredient in the transformation from information to intellectual asset is systemic information protection, a team effort where everyone contributes. Employees or other company stakeholders who are not actively protecting confidential information reduce your company's likelihood of transforming it into a trade secret asset.

Trade secrets are foundational to profiting from innovation. Patents are born from trade secrets, for example. Trade secrets give your company the legal right to sue to stop their unauthorized use and to be compensated for their loss or compromise.

Protecting information minimizes loss *and* enhances your company's legal position in case it is victim to trade secret misappropriation or theft. Your company may want to pursue legal recourse if another company, country, or person takes or uses its information without authorization. Under federal and state civil laws in the United States and in many other countries, as well as under international treaties, one who steals or uses trade secrets without authorization can be stopped, sent to jail, and forced to pay stiff penalties to the victim company. In all cases, however, the victim must first prove that the information taken and used without authorization is a trade secret. Without such proof, the victim has no recourse.

Because your company's information becomes a trade secret only if you and others with access apply reasonable efforts to protect it, the steps you take to protect information today may be the evidence your company needs in a future lawsuit. *U.S. v. Davis, No. 97-124 (M.D. Tennessee)* is one case that illustrates the importance of applying reasonable protection measures to establish trade secrets. The Gillette

Company hired Wright Industries, Inc., a fabrication equipment designer, to assist in developing a new shaving system. Steven Davis, a process controls engineer for Wright Industries who worked on the project, was angry at his supervisor. In retaliation for his grievances, he e-mailed and faxed Gillette's technical drawings to Warner-Lambert Co., Bic, and American Safety Razor Co., Gillette's competitors in the razor market. It is only because Gillette's employees collectively treated the information as confidential and Gillette required that its contractor, Wright Industries, do the same that Gillette was able to take action against Davis and Wright Industries. The U.S. federal prosecutors were successful in their criminal case against Davis, who was convicted of stealing more than $1.5 million worth of trade secrets.

When employees and other stakeholders generally abide by positively confidential practices, a security breach, such as a contractor offering to sell technical drawings to competitors, is easier to discover, prosecute, and resolve. Conversely, lax or inconsistent information protection may render a company powerless in the event of a costly and devastating information loss. In every trade secrets case, recourse against those who compromise confidential information depends on proving that individual stakeholders were working together to keep sensitive information from becoming known to competitors or to the public.

Avoiding a Lawsuit Is Better Than Winning One

Positioning your company to win a trade secrets lawsuit is a compelling reason to protect confidential information, but an even better one is to avoid lawsuits in the first place. Consider the case of Lexar and Toshiba. In April 1998, Lexar and Toshiba created a partnership to develop and manufacture flash memory chips. Soon afterward, Toshiba entered into a joint agreement and signed a $700 million deal to create a joint fabrication facility to produce flash memory chips with SanDisk, Lexar's main competitor. Feeling betrayed by Toshiba, Lexar suspected that Toshiba was using Lexar's intellectual property in its partnership with SanDisk.

Lexar did not have the proof until 2001 when Toshiba published the technical specifications used in its smart memory application. It was then clear to Lexar that Toshiba had used Lexar's intellectual property in developing the memory chips with SanDisk. Lexar sued Toshiba and was awarded $465.4 million in total damages, including $84 million in punitive damages, in 2005. While this award may appear large, it could not compensate Lexar for its time, litigation costs, distraction in the marketplace, and lost partnership with Toshiba. Had Lexar's and Toshiba's employees consistently protected their own company's secrets, both companies, as well as SanDisk, may have avoided this lengthy trial and the animosity it engendered.

Litigation is expensive, time-consuming, and distracting. Trade secret litigation is particularly so because emotions run high when people feel cheated by others who take and use information that they should not. Legal fees for trade secret litigation, especially if it ends in a trial, often run in the millions of dollars, and legal fees are only part of the total, and often astronomical, trade secret litigation costs. What would happen to your company's business relationships, sales, deals, and product announcements if headlines touted reports about a trial involving your company's lost information? Your company would find itself in a mess, with its reputation tarnished and a major distracter for you, your company, and your company's customers.

Even in criminal cases, where the state or federal government prosecutes, there are high costs to the victim company, including the time and money spent assisting with investigations. Sitting on the sidelines without control over how the case is handled can also be frustrating for the victim company stakeholders.

Protecting information helps avoid costly and aggravating lawsuits. When lawsuits are unavoidable, the steps taken to protect information can make the difference between an open-and-shut case and a long, drawn-out, nail-biting, financially-draining litigation that results in a disappointing outcome. Integrating a few simple steps into your job now helps you to avoid being derailed by lawsuits in the future.

Valuable Intellectual Property

The proliferation of information-based products and services generates many new revenue stream opportunities. Subscription-based software as a service, membership Web sites, know-how licensing, fee-based webinars, seminars, e-books, and audio or video DVDs are some of the many emerging possibilities for expanding offerings and income. Ordinary information must be transformed into intellectual property (patents, copyrights, and trade secrets) to make such money-making opportunities possible. Protecting information and thereby creating intellectual property also preserves for your company the option to commercialize it through licensure or trade for other intellectual property.

IBM is one of the best-known companies that protects its products and technologies and generates revenue by licensing its intellectual assets. The giant corporation has collected many billions of dollars from over forty thousand worldwide patents; IBM continues to be awarded thousands of new patents each year. As of 2010, it led the world in patents issued for seventeen consecutive years. This achievement is only possible because IBM is also a leader in protecting confidential information and trade secrets. Underlying and accompanying each patent, no matter who owns it, is an invention or discovery that is held secret until the patent is filed or issued or until it is licensed for profit.

The value of intellectual property is made abundantly clear by companies that do not make their money from producing the products or providing the services covered by their patents. Instead, these companies, sometimes referred to as "patent trolls," threaten lawsuits based on claims that others are infringing on their patents. While reviewing its patent portfolio, Forgent Networks came across U.S. Patent No. 4,698,672, which it obtained when it acquired Compression Labs in 1997. The patent purportedly gave Forgent the rights to the JPEG method for compressing digital images. The company, which received more than $100 million in fees from Adobe Systems, Macromedia, Yahoo!, and others, sued dozens of other companies, including Apple, Dell, IBM, and Microsoft, and won millions more. As with IBM's billions, Forgent Network's millions of dollars derived from patent licensing was only possible because all employees and stakeholders who had access to information about the inventions before they were patented kept that information confidential.

There is a direct relationship between you and your company's potential billion-dollar patent portfolio, regardless of your position in the company or job title. Twenty-first century information treasures are stored in your mind, computer, and mobile device hard drives. You may be tempted to post them on blogs, social networking sites, wikis, and online virtual worlds, such as Second Life®. They may pass through your hands as a hard copy or fax. You can communicate them via cell phone, text message, instant message, e-mail, or streaming Internet video. Valuable information sits on your desk by day and can be stuffed into your briefcase, backpack, or laptop bag in the evening. You review it on airplanes, discuss it over cocktails, and photocopy it at hotel business centers. Valuable information is sometimes embodied, but is often intangible. It is a product of the mind that can be stored as zeroes and ones, transmitted wirelessly, or divulged without words.

Wherever stored and however transmitted, you, as an information user, determine if it will hold the power and rewards of a secret or if its naked facts will become commonplace. It is up to you, and each individual company stakeholder, to keep information from your competitors and the public and to safeguard sensitive information against those whose use of it might diminish its worth or humiliate you or your company. By actively protecting information, you establish your company's ownership rights to its products, ideas, designs, processes, strategies, and other valuable data. You transform what you learn into valuable intellectual assets that can be defended and parlayed into profits.

Protecting information establishes it as proprietary, giving your company advantageous options. One option is to hold the information as your company's secret, creating a mystery that energizes business success. Another option may be to obtain a patent and license it for millions of dollars. All information is a potential intellectual asset and instantiated value. If you fail to protect it, you limit your company's options to benefit from it. Today, no one can afford to give away an intellectual asset unless there is a strategic reason for doing so.

Inappropriate Use of Confidential Information Can Be Devastating

Exposure can destroy secrets. Their potency and uniqueness can be lost forever with irreversible consequences. Sharing the results of your work via Facebook, a public Internet chat or blog, your avatar in Second Life, or posting to a Yahoo! Group's discussion negates confidentiality. The information becomes available for the taking. Your company loses rights to it, and you lose potential enrichment from your company having those rights. Similarly, if you reveal another person's private information inappropriately to even one person, it can destroy others' trust in your company. You cannot undo or recover from

- A leaked product announcement that allows a competitor to announce a new competing product one day before your company's planned product launch
- A customer who, upon discovering that someone in your company has been sloppy in handling his sensitive information, backs out of a business deal

Lost lead time, damaged reputations, diminished market differentiation, and decreased competitive advantages are costs of information loss that are often impossible to quantify. Some companies resort to measuring losses in terms of their cost to develop the information or the missed opportunity to license or sell it. Based on this calculation method, companies lose billions of dollars worth of proprietary information every year, often because of employee inadvertence that could have been avoided with just a little effort (see chapter 2).

In spring 2010, a soldier in the Israel Defense Forces posted the following status on his Facebook page, "On Wednesday we clean up Qatanah, and on Thursday, G-d willing, we come home." According to Haaretz.com, the online version of Israel's oldest daily newspaper, the soldier provided additional information, including the name of the combat unit, operation location, and time of the raid. His Facebook friends reported him to military authorities. As a result, the raid on the Palestinian territory was cancelled. The soldier did not comprehend that information about the timing and location of a planned military operation was confidential and that making it known, particularly on Facebook, could doom the operation to failure. One soldier's inappropriate disclosure put the entire unit and military mission at risk. The soldier, like many corporate citizens, did not understand the connection between his information disclosures and putting his and others' lives and livelihoods in danger.

You must know what information can be made available, to whom, and under what circumstances to create positive confidentiality. Your wise actions allow your company to disclose information strategically. You may disagree with upper management's decision to promote a senior manager to executive status, for instance, but generating rumors about the change is not constructive. (A private conversation with a company official may be useful, however.) Your company's decision to keep the management change secret until it can be announced publicly under the most favorable conditions depends on, and ultimately benefits, you.

Those who do not understand that discretion and tact are a fair exchange for the privilege of having access to information can easily cause egregious trouble. Consider this story from one of my clients, a financial services firm. An employee discovered that one of his neighbors, a customer of the firm, had an account with assets worth more than $1 million. While driving past his neighbor's house one day, the employee found the neighbor's lawn unkempt, and not for the first time. He sent the following well-intentioned e-mail:

> Hey, neighbor, your lawn is an eyesore and an embarrassment. I work with your financial services company and know you have more than $1 million in assets invested with us. Why don't you spend a few hundred dollars of that money fixing up your lawn? I'm sure the investment will improve our entire neighborhood's property values.

Luckily, the irate neighbor/customer complained directly to my client's company. He didn't send out the threatened blast of postings to Web sites that publish consumer grievances about financial services companies nor did he file the threatened complaint with the Securities and Exchange Commission (SEC). If the irate neighbor/customer had publicized the incident or filed a complaint with the SEC or if the incident had occurred after Gramm-Leach-Bliley (the United States federal law that requires financial services companies to ensure the security and confidentiality of customer data) was enacted, it is likely that the company would no longer exist. One incident involving a single imprudent employee using customer information improperly could have caused a well-respected and profitable company to fail.

How are these stories relevant to you? As a savvy and responsible professional, you understand it is best to avoid blunders that might cause your company to crash. You may assume that you are too smart or the likelihood of making such a miscalculation is too remote to worry about it. Many who have thought that way have been sadly mistaken; some have been terminated, sued, and even sent to prison.

Costly misjudgments can happen with regularity unless a positively confidential culture is a priority. Consider another headline-grabbing story where scientists at Merck reviewed study data about the connection between Vioxx and heart disease during the editorial stages leading to their final report. The word processing software was programmed to track their changes. Merck made the report available to the *New England Journal of Medicine*, unaware the metadata (the information about what had been added to and deleted from the report) was easily revealed. After the *New England Journal of Medicine* reported the metadata, lawsuits were filed against Merck, which ultimately withdrew Vioxx from the market and lost its opportunity for a multibillion-dollar globally-marketable product.

Doing a better job of concealing information about your company's potentially dangerous product is not the point. The story's takeaway is that, when you are dealing with your company's secrets, what you do and don't do *is* consequential. Every action or inaction has an effect and can have unintended and devastating outcomes. Inappropriate and misdirected conversations, e-mails, text messages, and metadata can destroy a career and a company.

An Ounce of Prevention May Be Worth Millions

It is your job to ensure that the valuable information you create, access, use, and share remains valuable to your company. Your thoughtful and consistent efforts to protect your company's confidential information can mean the difference between you and your company being a leader or an ill-fated also-ran.

By applying a positively confidential approach, you generate trust and confidence in those who share their information with you, help to build a profitable company, and avoid the pain of damage control later. Implementing information safeguards is an offensive tactic that creates merit and contributes to realizing your company's fullest potential, as well as a defensive action to avoid costly losses and embarrassment.

If you protect information, you gain more than the effort you put in. If you don't protect information, you lose much more than it takes to avoid loss. You enhance your own value and further your career by protecting information because, the savvier you are at it, the more you enhance your company's financial well-being, positive future, and value of your available stock options.

Protecting information is easy, particularly when every employee does her part. Yes, it takes a moment to type "confidential" in the footer of a proposal you are sending to a customer, and it requires restraint not to blurt out your company's next-generation product details when your time is taken up with little else. Passwords can be bothersome, too, especially when you have to remember several and must change them periodically. Walking to the copy room to shred a confidential budget draft may be inconvenient. Yet these are not merely administrative burdens that take extra steps, work, or time. They are part of your job, your responsibility, *and* your opportunity to do your job better by creating positive confidentiality that helps your company thrive.

Chapter 1 Spot Quiz
Know Why Protecting Information Matters

(The answer key can be found in appendix D)

Your information protection efforts support which of the following aspirations of your organization?

A. Marketing punch

B. Great reputation

C. Customer confidence

D. Trust

E. All of the above

Is the following statement true or false?

Although protecting intellectual property is not one of your job responsibilities, you should adhere to information protection principles to earn a pat on the back.

Understand the Risks
of Not Protecting Information

CHAPTER 2

Chapter 2 Takeaways

What are the risks?

- Loose lips (and other forms of information sharing) can sink your company's ship.

- Information scouts are everywhere, eager to take advantage of you.

- You and other well-meaning employees, contractors, vendors, and customers are easy targets if unaware of the risks.

Loose Lips Sink Ships

The world War II-era slogan "Loose lips sink ships," had both literal and metaphorical significance. During the war, if you were careless about what you said or to whom you said it, you could literally reveal the information needed to sink a ship. Today, you can metaphorically sink the enterprise for which you work, and, with it, the hopes and aspirations, including stock options, bonuses, sales commissions, career advancement, job security, and other benefits, of all those who work with you.

Consider, for example, the wreckage a friendly businessman caused on an airplane flight home. A technical manager from a medical device company was flying between Boston, Massachusetts, and San Jose, California, when he overheard a man sitting across the aisle talking to his seatmate. The listener's ears perked up when he realized the freely chatting man worked for a direct competitor. The conversant passenger was overtly frustrated about the technical complications his company was facing while launching a new product. At the end of an hour, the listener knew his competitor's price, the malfunctions of the medical device, and the product's first and anchor customer.

As soon as he disembarked, the accidental spy called his sales director to convey the details. The salesman immediately set to work to eliminate the competition. He met with the competitor's anchor customer and undercut the competitor's price, pointed out the flaws in the competitor's product, and won a contract for the new medical device, all based on information his co-worker overheard on the airplane. Because the anchor customer was pivotal for winning more business, the company that lost the customer was never able to gain traction for its new product. The company with the loose-lipped employee was out of business within eighteen months.

As this story illustrates, it takes only one inadvertent confidential information disclosure for an entire company—its competitive advantages, market share, technology leadership, and the trust of its customers—to be destroyed. A potentially lethal leak—intentional or accidental—could comprise just a single information tidbit remarked to an unknown telephone solicitor, e-mailed to someone who does not need it, or diagrammed and left on a whiteboard when the room is unattended.

When your company's valuable information gets into the wrong hands, there is incalculable potential harm even if the result is not total destruction of your organization. Imagine, for example, your competitors having access to your company's strategic plans, product launch plans, beta customers' evaluation results, new product formulas, manufacturing processes, budgets, or marketing strategies.

Your competitors could, as in the case of the airline traveler, use the information to defeat you. Or they might just tell your customers what you did not want them to know or inform a journalist who makes public the secrets of your previous triumph. The harm is in squandering the time, money, effort, and resources invested in that information. The cost is in losing the profits whose potential rested in that confidential information. The injury is also to your own pride in your company as it suffers from a tainted reputation. Information loss will eliminate bragging rights in what was formerly unique to your company. The price of such a loss reverses the payback on your labor as competitors make gains.

In another seemingly innocent incident, an employee interested in keeping his job options open posted his résumé on the Internet; it included a brief description of his current employer's top-secret project. A competitor that actively scanned for résumés from competitors discovered it. The competitor was able to use the information to improve its own similar new product and then beat the employer with it. The employer lost its competitive lead and its ability to patent its product. The employee who caused the loss did not get a job or any benefit from the competitor. Instead, the competitor disrespected him because he disclosed sensitive information in his résumé. He remained with his current employer, who became less competitive because of the information loss.

Information Loss Opportunities Are Abundant and Cost Amply

Imagine a company with one thousand employees where each employee has twenty daily business interactions, totaling twenty thousand business interactions per day in the company. If just 5 percent of those interactions involve confidential information (a very conservative percentage for most companies), there are one thousand instances of confidential information sharing per day for this hypothetical company, leading to one thousand opportunities each business day to take or steal confidential information. If in just 1 percent of those instances a person exposes the information to someone who uses it for her own benefit and not the company's best interests, a one-thousand-employee company has ten incidents every business day where its valuable information is compromised. Under these circumstances, the company diminishes its competitive advantage, decreases its market share, disgraces its business relationships, and degrades its reputation ten times a day.

Multiply this information loss potential by the number of employees, contractors, vendors, and others who can access your company's confidential information. What you get is a conservative estimate of the number of instances each day when your company's information treasures are at risk, possibly devalued, or lost completely.

Calculation of Confidential Information Exposures Per Day Per 1,000 Employees

Factors	Calculation
Employees	1,000
Daily business interactions per employee	20
Total daily interactions for the company	20,000
Percent involving confidential information	5%
Daily potential exposures of confidential information	1,000
Percent of interactions that result in loss or compromise if confidential information is not protected	1%
Number of instances of valuable confidential information compromised each day per 1,000 employees	10

Table 2

As early as 1998, a study conducted by the American Society for Industrial Security projected that U.S.-based companies lose approximately $50 billion worth of trade secrets each year. In another study that same year, the Computer Security Institute, in conjunction with the FBI, found that the average annual information loss suffered by those companies who could quantify it was $1.67 million.

Both the American Society for Industrial Security and the Computer Security Institute, as well as several other organizations, have conducted more recent studies that continue to find that, using the traditional methods of quantifying information loss, American companies are losing billions of dollars worth of valuable information each year. Still, these figures do not account for the added, and measurable, costs of legal action (chapter 1). If your company loses information or it is stolen and your company wants to file a lawsuit to protect its interests, the costs are enormous. In 2010, the average cost of trade secret litigation was $1.5 million per case in hard dollar costs. There are many other intangible costs, not the least of which is diverting the engineers, scientists, and salespeople from developing and selling your company's products and services to dealing with litigation.

In 2005, ChoicePoint admitted that suspected criminals passing themselves off as legitimate customers accessed its database of consumer records. The Federal Trade Commission (FTC) reported that the financial data of 163,000 people were exposed in the breach, and at least 800 cases of identity theft arose from it.

ChoicePoint was in the business of providing consumer data services to insurance companies and government agencies, among other organizations. They maintained about 19 billion personal records of U.S. residents, including consumers' names, addresses, Social Security numbers, birth dates, and credit reports. Organizations paid to access ChoicePoint's data in order to create background profiles on customers applying for loans, insurance, or government jobs. As one can imagine, not just valid organizations wanted ChoicePoint's consumer information. Thieves also wanted it to create phony bank and credit accounts and to transfer and withdraw money.

Perpetrators duped ChoicePoint employees by pretending to be qualified purchasers of consumer data. They set up fifty fraudulent accounts with ChoicePoint by posing as businesses, such as collection agencies, that were looking to run background checks on their potential customers. The criminals used previously stolen identities to set up what appeared to be lawful business licenses, phone numbers, and addresses for the organizations they claimed to be working for when applying for accounts.

There were clues, though, that something was amiss. Some subscribers applied for accounts using commercial mail drops as business addresses. Some sent multiple faxed applications from the same fax number or business address, with each form listing the sender as a different business. The ChoicePoint employees responsible for account creation did not see these clues because, like most workers, the ChoicePoint employees handling the transactions were more focused on providing good customer service and helping their company grow. Their actions were inconsistent with the company's public statements: "ChoicePoint allows access to your consumer reports only by those authorized." "Every ChoicePoint customer must successfully complete a rigorous credentialing process."

On September 27, 2004, ChoicePoint first discovered that a few of its small business customers in the Los Angeles area were engaged in "suspicious activity." Initially, the company notified law enforcement agencies. Then, in February 2005, as required by state law, the company notified thirty-five thousand California residents that their records were improperly accessed. After a public outcry for more information, the company notified an additional 110,000 American citizens that they were victims of the same problem.

Following the incident, the FTC, SEC, Los Angeles County Sheriff's Department, a number of state attorneys general, and several congressional leaders launched investigations into various aspects of ChoicePoint's operations. The FTC charged ChoicePoint with violating the Fair Credit Reporting Act and making false and misleading statements about its privacy policies. Under the settlement agreement, ChoicePoint was ordered to obtain independent assessments of its data security program every year through 2026. ChoicePoint had to pay $10 million in civil penalties to the FTC. ChoicePoint was also compelled to provide $5 million to recompense consumers who suffered because of ChoicePoint's actions. The company reported $2 million in additional charges to notify victims of the incident and $9.4 million in legal and professional fees.

These aren't the only consequences of the case. ChoicePoint's business had been selling aggregated consumer information. Instead of being able to focus on marketing and selling its products and services, it spent more than a year working with federal, state, and local law enforcement officials on resolving the case.

After the SEC's inquiry into its business practices, ChoicePoint exited some significant segments of its business, which was projected to cost the company $15 to $20 million in sales during 2005 alone and reduce earnings that year by 10 to 12 cents per share. On top of these distractions and losses, the company faced a tidal wave of lawsuits accusing it of fraud and negligence for its alleged inability to protect consumers' private data.

ChoicePoint's press relations staff had to apologize to consumers that may have been affected by the fraudulent activity. They tried to reestablish credibility for ChoicePoint's commitment to protect personal data. In the wake of the storm, however, they were backpedaling and not moving the company forward. In 2008, Anglo-Dutch publishing company Reed Elsevier acquired ChoicePoint.

An important lesson from this case is that if you are not aware of the prevalence of information robbers you will likely be duped, just like the employees at ChoicePoint who thought that providing good service and growing their company were more important than being vigilant about protecting information. Like the ChoicePoint employees, you can also inadvertently cause catastrophic damage to your company. Your failure to protect information could result in turning the successful organization for whom you work into an icon of distrust. This could happen to anyone who is not careful.

Information Scouts Are Everywhere

How could you—a smart, professional, and respected employee—wreak such havoc on your company? You are capable of causing devastation because others are listening. In wartime, the enemy listens at every opportunity to any hint of what the opponent is doing, as well as how, when, with whom, and where. In the business world, the competitor, vendor, business partner, and customer is listening from the seat behind you in the airplane, directing questions to you at an industry conference, seeking your perspective on next-generation products, or requesting your participation in a study.

We are all vulnerable to being flattered, intellectually engaged, and seduced into divulging sensitive information. Or, as often happens, we could provide a nonconfidential piece of information that, together with other pieces of information, reveals company trade secrets. Why shouldn't you trust the person requesting information from you? She assures you that she does not want you to violate any obligation you have to keep your company's confidential information secret. And it's true. She does not want to ask for confidential information from you because she knows that, if she were to ask for it directly, you might not give it to her. She instead asks you for one piece of her puzzle. By itself, the information she seeks from you is not confidential. The information she receives from one of your company's vendors, by itself, may also be nonconfidential. Her Google search reveals additional relevant information, as does the transcript of a recent speech that your company's CEO gave at an investor conference. While none of these sources individually disclose your organization's business strategy, new product direction, or marketing plans, together, they can paint a very illuminating picture. Your conversation with the woman who requested nonconfidential information may provide her the final missing puzzle piece (see figure1).

Completing Their Puzzle With Your Piece of Information

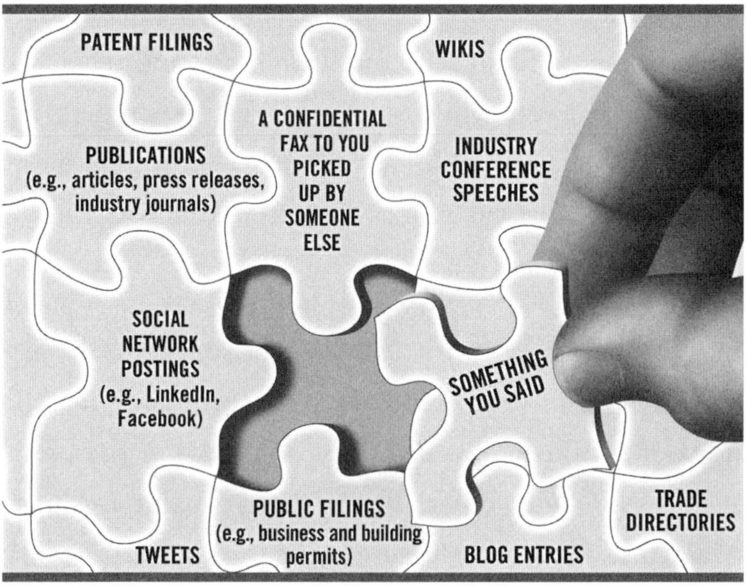

PATENT FILINGS

WIKIS

PUBLICATIONS
(e.g., articles, press releases,
industry journals)

A CONFIDENTIAL
FAX TO YOU
PICKED
UP BY
SOMEONE
ELSE

INDUSTRY
CONFERENCE
SPEECHES

SOCIAL
NETWORK
POSTINGS
(e.g., LinkedIn,
Facebook)

SOMETHING
YOU SAID

TWEETS

PUBLIC FILINGS
(e.g., business and building
permits)

BLOG ENTRIES

TRADE
DIRECTORIES

Figure 1

Because nonconfidential information can be aggregated to reveal confidential information, the opportunities to cause your company harm are abundant and ubiquitous, particularly in today's global, technologically-advanced, mobile, and interconnected business environment. Competitors, customers, vendors, business partners, industry analysts, and the press all want to know your company's secrets. They seek out the secrets themselves and hire business intelligence firms to find them. Most use smart, trained, shrewd people to get confidential information from you using legal means. Some may follow you at a trade show; others will follow your postings on blogs, social networking sites, and online chat groups.

Some will use illegal means to get information from you. They will steal your laptop at the airport, intercept the confidential fax sent to you at an international hotel, or plant a microphone in the conference room where you are holding a confidential meeting. They will hack into your laptop via your wireless port when you are on the road. They will infect your computer with spyware when you are at home and use it to get passwords that will unlock the networks at your office.

Some technically- and socially-sophisticated thieves obtain information in ways that simply stretch the line between what is legal and ethical. They ignore your ever-present confidentiality marking and forward your confidential e-mail to a competitor or the press. They ignore the "No Photographs, Please" sign in your manufacturing facility and use their cell phone camera to take snapshots of your manufacturing equipment. They invite you back for extended job interviews long after they know you are not the right person for a job, which may or may not really exist, so they can ask you for more information about what you do, what you think, and how you would solve their problems based on your experience working for your current employer.

Information scouts—legal and illegal, ethical and unethical—are everywhere. They are eager to read your e-mail and online postings, listen to your conversations, and get a copy of your work product. They are keen to take advantage of what you know and anticipate your next move.

You May Be the Best Target

Picture a team member. He's ready to help, wanting to please, and excited to collaborate with colleagues, familiar and new, to build a great company. What does that make him? An easy and vulnerable target.

Why? That employee has firsthand knowledge about his employer. Depending on his position, he might also have firsthand knowledge about what others are doing. Such knowledge is the most accurate and sought-after information available. The employee also has opinions, perspectives, and contributions to make to the world in which we live. He has a sense of pride about what his organization is working on or possibly a newfound gripe about something your company's management does or does not do. His desire to please makes him susceptible to being conned by someone interested in what he knows, thinks, or feels. He is human.

This person could be a friend of yours; he could even be you. When someone takes a genuine interest in you and the work you do, you are likely to respond. For most of us, it is a gift when someone demonstrates sincere curiosity about what we do and know. We tend to engage in conversation—online and offline—in response to a person's attention and interest gratuity. The adage "Flattery will get you everywhere" describes a situation that happens to the least suspecting of dedicated employees.

Victor Lee was an engineer working for Avery Dennison in 1989 when the Industrial Technology Research Institute (ITRI) invited him to Taiwan to give a lecture. Representatives of Four Pillars Enterprises who attended the ITRI lecture requested that he give the same lecture at their company. Mr. Lee was then asked to work as a "secret consultant" for Four Pillars. From 1989 to 1997, Mr. Lee was paid $150,000 to $160,000 through various channels for supplying Avery Dennison's trade secret technology to Four Pillars. Avery Dennison estimated $60 million in losses from Four Pillars' arrangement with Mr. Lee. While

Mr. Lee eventually cooperated with FBI investigators, he pled guilty to wire fraud and was sentenced to a one-year detention for his role in the unlawful scheme. Four Pillars was found guilty of conspiracy and attempted trade secret theft. In a subsequent civil trial, Avery Dennison was awarded $60 million to compensate the company for trade secret misappropriation, conversion, and other violations. Victor Lee was liable, with Four Pillars, to pay the damages award.

The Avery Dennison affair brings into sharp focus the kind of attention and allure to be wary of, particularly if you are traveling on company business and have access to coveted intellectual property. Jet-lagged and lonely in some distant city, perhaps worrying about never-ending bills or past due taxes over a drink or two, you might be approached and tantalized with a quick cash fix. You know that crime does not pay, just as Victor Lee may have known and certainly knows now, yet enticement can be a perilous cocktail.

You may never be approached by an international firm offering to pay you hundreds of thousands of dollars in consulting fees in exchange for your company's trade secrets. Still, anyone may be tempted to steal and leak confidential information. In January 2010, Gawker Media started a "scavenger hunt" requesting any exclusive photos, video, or samples of Apple Computer's unreleased new iPad™ tablet, offering a $100,000 prize for the first person to provide them with access to the product. Perhaps because Apple is known for keeping product information secret until just before releases, fans, bloggers, and other members of the media spend hours poring over tiny bits of information that might provide clues to the next big thing Apple is developing.

You may have only limited access to details about unreleased products or how your company, or another company, succeeds today or what it plans for tomorrow. Still, with your firsthand knowledge, a good head on your shoulders, and natural instincts to respond to those interested in what you know and do, you and the other well-meaning people you talk to and correspond with—for example, fellow employees, contractors, vendors, and customers—are easy targets for turning your company into a loser unless you know and address the risks.

Competitive Intelligence Professionals, Industrial Spies, and Hackers

It's you against thousands of savvy, flattering, bright, interesting, and interested people who keep getting better at extracting information from you without you even being aware of it. And it's not just curious competitors interested in the tempting tidbits of information they may overhear at a trade show, but a battalion of really intelligent, sophisticated, adept information gatherers actively looking for intelligent, engaging, thoughtful people, just like you. In fact, if you work with sensitive company information, whether it be in research and development, marketing, product development, sales, manufacturing, information technology, facilities, security, procurement, finance, or business strategy, it is highly likely that a competitive intelligence professional is specifically targeting you and gathering corroborating information from your colleagues, customers, business partners, suppliers, contractors, student interns, industry analysts, and the press.

These competitive intelligence professionals who regularly gather corporate information using legal means have a slew of organizations catering to honing their skills. Associations such as the Society of Competitive Intelligence Professionals, which boasted more than three thousand members in 2010, provide seminars to teach interviewing and interrogation techniques that promise attendees the skills to get information "like an expert pickpocket."

One big difference is that, when the pickpocket has stolen something valuable, the victim eventually discovers that it is missing. Not so when information is taken. A good competitive intelligence professional never leaves you feeling violated. Instead, you feel clever, helpful, and productive, although your intellectual pocket has been picked. And while firsthand information is most valuable, collecting it is not the only method a competitive intelligence professional uses to get at your company's secrets. These clue gatherers also look at what you do, where you go, and with whom you meet.

A competitive intelligence professional has the skills to read your business strategy from the tea leaves of information you and your company make available. The names on the trucks entering your company's facilities, employees' postings on social networking sites, new ideas presented at trade shows by your vendors, and those last validating comments you provided in response to questions from a "student researcher" are hints and pointers. Competitive intelligence professionals are proficient at putting these pieces of information together to form a mosaic of their target company's strategies and tactics.

It is likely that your own company has a competitive intelligence professional on staff. Check it out. Is there someone listed in your personnel directory whose title includes business analyst, market analyst, strategic business intelligence, or competitive intelligence? Who in your company responds to inquiries about your company's business or market plans and strategies? Bear in mind that your company and its competitors are not limited to gathering and analyzing useful information through internal intelligence resources. Hundreds of firms specialize in collecting and studying business, market, finance, strategy, and competitive intelligence. These firms thrive because your company's competitors are willing to pay millions of dollars for the secrets of your company's success.

Competitive intelligence professionals (those who gather information using legal means) and spies (those who gather information using illegal means) are not the only ones targeting you for valuable information. Computer hackers know well that the weakest links in the chain of an organization's security system are people. In one case, a hired hacker was able to quickly access a company's network because employees had used easy-to-guess passwords, for example, the words on their personalized license plates. Many hackers will obtain passwords to gain sensitive information on a company's network by using a ruse, sometimes referred to as social engineering (when made by telephone) or phishing (when made by e-mail).

The pitch might go something like this:

> Hi, my name is Sally, and I'm working with IT Security Services. We are implementing a policy that will require stronger passwords and access controls. I'm calling to see if your network password meets our policy requirements. How often do you change your password? What network password do you currently use?

If you received such a call in the course of a busy day or night, and a confident professional directed these questions at you, would you provide your password? If your honest answer is yes, you are not alone.

In 2007, auditors from the United States Treasury Inspector General for Tax Administration Office (TIGTA) conducted a test where they telephoned employees and contractors at the Internal Revenue Service (IRS). Pretending to be IRS help desk workers, the auditors asked the IRS employees and contractors to provide their user names and to temporarily change their passwords to one that the auditor specified. While the individuals might not have given away their own secret password, 60 percent of those telephoned complied with the request and changed their password to the one provided to them. The result was, of course, the same because these IRS employees and contractors forfeited the keys to the IRS network by changing their password to the one suggested to them. A similar test in 2004 netted just 35 percent. In 2001, 71 percent changed their passwords. That test prompted corrective actions designed to increase awareness of social engineering tactics. The most recent test involved 102 employees. Just eight of the people who received telephone calls responded appropriately by contacting the audit team, the TIGTA Office of Investigators, or the IRS computer security organization.

Many people will listen to stories of successful social engineering attacks and think, "I would never be that gullible. How could someone fall for such an obvious scam?" Well, unless you train yourself to detect and resist social engineering attacks, if—or more likely when—you are targeted, you won't be expecting it. It will be disarming. The request-or's justification will seem plausible. It will work on your emotions or thought processes in a way that you had not anticipated, or it might even manifest as something so trivial or routine that it does not register on your radar screen. Will you be ready? Many are not.

Not Just You and Your Fellow Employees

Incident after incident shows that the keys to a company's kingdom are often available to outsiders who simply ask for them, and there are so many people to ask. Think of all those other than you and your fellow employees who can access your company's valuable information: transitory employees, contractors, consultants, vendors, student interns, customers, business partners, and seasonal workers, including those who support your core business functions and those who provide janitorial, cafeteria, floral decor, security, and other office facility support. Every day, you work with trusted outsiders. Even the most loyal and best-intentioned of these will likely want to use the information accessible to them to promote themselves for their next potential business opportunity. Contractors, consultants, and temporaries are constantly tempted to tell their new prospects and customers about their last customer's challenges and solutions as a way of establishing their credibility.

Anyone interested in information about you or your firm might also target the contractors, consultants, vendors, student interns, customers, and business partners who work for your company's contractors, consultants, vendors, customers, and business partners (see figure 2).

Those Seeking a Company's Confidential Information Have a Broad and Rich Target Area

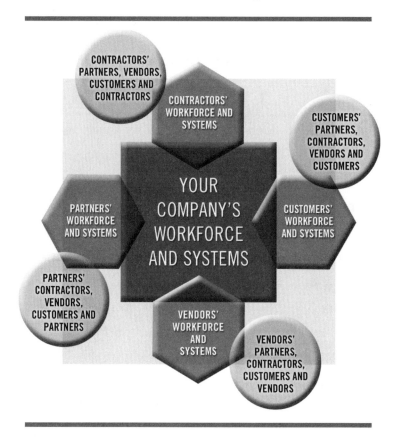

Figure 2

In our global economy, business partners include outsourced product developers and offshore manufacturers. Our information-sharing network also includes family members, friends, and other confidants of each individual who have access to a company's confidential information. It is an abundant, worldwide network of people eager to share their thoughts in response to a telephone call or an e-mail inquiry, in a blog or listserv, or at a webinar, conference, or trade show.

Do you remember our hypothetical example of the one thousand-employee company that has ten likely incidents of information loss each day? The number of stakeholders with access to information from extended, interconnected organizations multiplies the number of likely incidents exponentially.

The Missing Puzzle Piece

Because there are so many people in your company's extended enterprise and other sources of information are so prevalent, the small bits of additional information that you provide may be precisely what an outsider needs to complete an accurate picture of your company's strengths and vulnerabilities (figure 1).

Whatever you reveal is added to the rich information that can be pulled together from your company's Web site, discussions with your company's vendors, presentations by company engineers or scientists at technical conferences, industry associations, blogs focused on your industry, company, or products, and your fellow employees' YouTube and social networking postings. The information available is sometimes unimaginable. You might want to ask your company's competitive intelligence professional to share with you the picture she has put together of your competitors based on research from open sources.

All that may be missing from your competitor's understanding of your company's plans and frailties is a confirmation from you—what seems to you like a general statement of your personal conjecture. Nothing confidential there, right? Perhaps. Nevertheless, the resulting narrative may be one you never intended to divulge.

Kara, a member of a business intelligence team from "Bray Inc.," was able to gather the puzzle pieces she needed from unsuspecting temporary contract employees. Kara was assigned the task of mapping the corporate organizations of Bray's primary competitors so Bray's executives could anticipate and defeat them. The mapping exercise included detailed explanations of each competitor's executives' personalities for use by Bray's human resources department to recruit the best of these competitors' employees to Bray.

Kara discovered a Web site providing a wiki (software that allows users to create a collaborative Web site) for company organization charts. Using what she found on that site as a starting point, Kara developed her own organization charts of previously identified competitors' companies. She sent her initial version to Bray's senior managers with a request that they add to or correct any outdated information that they found in her charts. Then Kara asked the human resources department to notify her when temporary employees came to work for Bray. Kara would visit with each temporary employee and say, "I have a high-paying permanent position in my department. I need someone with a good understanding of how different companies work. Your experience as a contract temporary employee would be well suited for this position."

She then asked questions such as

- Which other companies have you worked for?
- In which departments did you work?
- Who was your supervisor? To whom did she report?
- What were your supervisors' titles?
- What were they like?

After speaking with a temporary employee or other contractor, she was able to add information to her organization charts about competitors' employees, including their names, titles, lengths of service, and work philosophies. Within a few months, Kara developed a complete corporate organizational map and database of personalities describing each of Bray's primary competitors. Completing the competitor human resource map was possible only by aggregating the bits of information she received from Bray's temporary employees and other contractors. Once complete, Kara successfully used it to recruit her competitors' top talent.

The "Oops" Factor

Once you divulge information, your option to control it is easily lost. Perhaps you have answered a question sent to you via a text message, an instant message, or e-mail. After hitting the send button, you wished you hadn't. Perhaps you disclosed more than you should have to someone who did not need the information, or you blurted out some sensitive information without it being solicited. Worse yet, perhaps you posted it to a public forum such as a Twitter feed, the default of which makes everything publicly readable and searchable.

In stress or anger, after a little too much to drink, or in exhaustion or frivolity, anyone can err. Once you hit the send key, the information is gone, and it is irretrievable. If you hang up after leaving a voicemail message, you will not be able to delete it. Once you send a document via fax, you cannot recall it. If you boast of something at a party some night, no matter what promises of discretion you elicit the next morning, you cannot know for certain that the information will be kept secret.

Online Amplification

Online activity is particularly dicey. Technology, or rather, a lack of understanding about it, can betray you. Information you reveal under circumstances that seem obscure, such as a blog for golfers, listserv for working mothers, or an avatar on Second Life, is not hidden. It shows up easily using Web search technologies, including search technologies for archived Web pages and postings you thought were taken down.

If you tweet or post and remove the posted information later, others may still have a log. One executive at a major high-tech company accidentally posted to his public Twitter feed a reply to someone who had privately messaged him about a possible product flaw. He included his direct telephone number in his reply. Although he later removed the tweet from his public feed, many users following him had the information in their Twitter histories.

Most companies monitor the Internet for information about their company and competitors. A person responsible for such monitoring invariably utilizes automatic services, such as those offered by Google, Thomson Reuters, LexisNexis, and others that may be more sophisticated. Hundreds of public and private search engines continuously scour online data. The search services send e-mail notices whenever a company's name, one of its brands, or other vital keyword is used either in the blogosphere, general flow of Web sites, or news online. Nothing is too obscure for these searches. They find everything you wrote about your company, your work, and your perspectives on your employer's business.

The point is not to make you paranoid, although a healthy dose of caution is certainly appropriate. Nor should you stop sharing confidential information for purposes that benefit your organization. As we will explore in chapter 5, there are many good reasons to share confidential information that must be balanced with the equally good reasons to protect it.

The Most Significant Threat Is the Inadvertent One

If you are not keenly aware of omnipresent information loss risks, you increase them. The dominant hazard to a company's information and intellectual property is the inadvertent disclosure of valuable information by those who may not understand how important it is to protect it. During my twenty-five-year tenure of working with hundreds of companies, I have surveyed thousands of corporate citizens to determine the biggest threat to confidential information. Over the decades and around the world, an estimated 80 to 95 percent of confidential information loss is due to employee and other stakeholder inadvertence, not sabotage, and this has stayed constant.

You can reduce ubiquitous and avoidable losses by raising your awareness and helping to raise others' awareness of information loss risks. Caution, together with informed discretion, will minimize the likelihood that you will be tricked into revealing valuable information or falsely believing that the information you make known is safe.

Chapter 2 Spot Quiz
Understanding the Risks of Not Protecting Information

(The answer key can be found in appendix D)

Which of the following is the most prevalent threat to your company's confidential information?

A. Hackers breaking into the computer networks and stealing information from servers

B. Competitive intelligence professionals searching through all available public information looking for your company's secrets

C. Industrial spies conducting illegal electronic surveillance of your executives' communications

D. Well-meaning employees exposing confidential information inadvertently

Is the following statement true or false?

Information scouts only target scientists, engineers, and executives; that is, those with direct access to trade secrets and future business plans. Unless you have a job working with highly sensitive information, you are not likely to be targeted.

Identify the Information
You Need to Protect

CHAPTER 3

Chapter 3 Takeaways

What information do you need to protect?

- Protect all information that
  - your organization defines as confidential
  - others entrust to your organization subject to nondisclosure obligations
  - is private, personally identifiable information subject to privacy laws

- Protect only the information that needs protecting because overprotection can confuse, waste resources, and negate efforts.

What Do You Think Is Confidential?

Many consider information about their personal earnings to be private and confidential and to be shared only as needed with financial professionals (an accountant, investment manager, or taxing authorities, such as the IRS). But not my client Bill who directed corporate security for a large telecommunications company. As I walked with him after a meeting one day, he pointed to a car in the street and said, "Now that's a beautiful driving machine. But on my $110,000 annual salary, I'm sure it's not in my budget, even when you consider that my wife makes $75,000 a year."

I told Bill that he seemed unusually frank about his and his wife's salaries. He responded by telling me, "Before working in corporate security, I was in the army, where my compensation was publicly known. I got used to the idea that salaries were discussed candidly, and it's an effort for me to be secret about my current position's compensation." Bill's previous work experience, family background, and cultural upbringing all likely shaped Bill's approach to confidentiality and privacy.

Similarly, while many consider body weight and eating habits to be very personal and confidential, my former gym colleagues did not. I attended an aerobics class where the same fifteen women came early each Monday-Wednesday-Friday morning to workout. It was not unusual to overhear discussions in the locker room about what these women ate, their weight, their struggles sticking with a diet, and the size of their clothes. The information shared was often detailed and explicit. Neither the women participating in these chats nor those of us who could easily overhear them censured discussing such private matters openly. Camaraderie, the intimacy of the locker room, and the communal exercise experience probably influenced the women's sensitivity to privacy and confidentiality.

These two examples reflect choices that individuals make about their personal information. As owners of the information, they can choose to share or keep it secret. Neither choice is right or wrong. Based on these examples, can you determine if the following business information is confidential?

- The salary and benefits package associated with your job position
- Your need for handicapped parking
- Your company's business plan
- The names of your company's customers

The answer to each is, "It depends."

The Big "IF"

Information is confidential if the person or company who owns it decides it is confidential and takes steps to protect it. In the first example above, Bill shared both his and his wife's salary information openly by choice. Assuming Bill's disclosure was not a violation of his or his wife's company's rules, sharing wage information without restriction made it not confidential. My aerobics classmates in the locker room similarly shared information about their weight, diets, and clothing sizes openly. Because they did so without any attempt to prevent those who overheard them from sharing it further, the information was not confidential.

Your company's business plans, marketing strategies, product specifications, employee lists, packaging costs, and customer purchasing preferences may be confidential or not depending on the decisions of people in your company who are authorized to make the determination. The very act of identification is the first step in transforming it to confidential information.

If business information is not recognized as confidential, it will not be protected. It will be available to all those individuals, companies, and governments interested in taking it and using it to their advantage.

Sorting Information Types

Your organization has a lot of information, and you and other employees created some of it. Contractors developed other information.

Customers and business partners generated some and entrusted it to your company. More still was gathered electronically from visitors to your company's Web site or those who posted comments to your company's blogs or added content to its wikis, corporate Facebook page, or other online communities.

You might think that, with all this potentially valuable information floating around, it might be easiest to avoid sorting and just regard everything as confidential. But everything is not confidential. For example, the location of your company's holiday party, the size of your office windows, and the number of chairs in the lobby of your corporate headquarters are likely not confidential. If you don't differentiate what is confidential from what is not, you water down the distinctiveness of confidential information. And while protecting information can be achieved easily by applying the ten steps described in this book, it is a waste to apply that effort to information that can or should be freely shared.

To sort out all the various information types and determine what is confidential, it is helpful to take a brief look at each kind of information that your company possesses.

Your Organization's Information

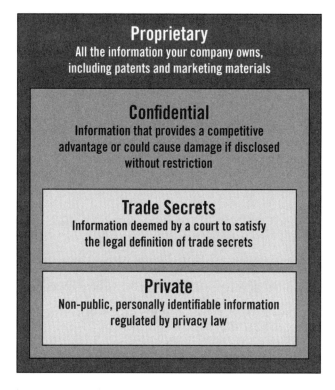

Figure 3

Proprietary Information

The broadest scope of information your company possesses is proprietary information. The term "proprietary" is based on the root word "proprietor," which means "owner" or "one who has the legal right or exclusive title to something."

Your company owns all of the information it develops and all of the information to which it acquires legal rights. Your company probably also possesses proprietary information owned by others. Not all of the information your company and other companies own is confidential.

Proprietary information also consists of information that the owner wants to share openly or is required to make public. For example, your company generally wants to share promotional material freely and does not treat it as confidential or restrict its distribution. In fact, with social media becoming a larger part of corporate marketing strategy, companies are pushing out promotional content through blogs, Facebook, LinkedIn, Twitter, YouTube, Flickr, and a whole host of other online tools. "Viral marketing," where news about a company and its products or services spreads like a virus, can create buzz and market traction that reaches a wide and expanding audience.

Marketing information can also be time-sensitive, benefiting your company only if it is released on a certain date or even at a specific time. If you are holding the nominations for the next Academy Awards, the details of a major acquisition, or a startling piece of investigative reporting, you will want to keep tight control of it so it is not leaked before its appointed time for public release. Such information can and should be treated as confidential until it is published. Once published, it may still be proprietary (owned by your company) but no longer confidential.

In most cases, proprietary information that your company wants to make public, such as advertisements, Web site content, or content posted by employees to company-sponsored blogs, is protected by copyright laws. Copyright laws provide your company with the exclusive right to reproduce, prepare derivative works based on, perform or display literary, musical, dramatic, pictorial, graphic, or other similar works publicly and authorize others to do the same.

Patents are an example of proprietary information that your company owns but cannot keep confidential. A patent is the exclusive right granted to an inventor by a national government to prevent others from making, using, selling, offering to sell, or importing that invention. Once a patent is filed, all patent claims are included in the public record, except under limited circumstances. Such information is part of your company's nonconfidential proprietary information, which your organization cannot protect from disclosure.

Confidential Information

Confidential information is a class of proprietary information that excludes publicly available information and is broader in scope than what a court may ascertain to be a trade secret. Confidential information can be broadly defined to include any information that might provide your company with a competitive advantage or be potentially damaging if it is disclosed without restriction. This broad definition encompasses all of the bits and pieces of information that competitive intelligence professionals might use to make inferences about your company's strategies or tactics. The definition also includes all of the information your company receives from its business partners and customers under nondisclosure obligations and agreements. Because confidential information can include any information that, if disclosed without restriction, could be harmful to your company, it also encompasses private and personally identifiable information. A sample inventory of confidential information is in appendix A, "Confidential Information Examples." You should use it as a guide only if your company does not have its own confidential information listing or inventory.

If your company has not made a listing of its confidential information, you can suggest that one be developed. If a list exists but seems outdated or incomplete, you might remind the person responsible for developing and disseminating it that it should be kept current and as complete as possible.

Trade Secrets

Just as confidential information is a subset of your company's proprietary information, trade secret information is a subset of your company's confidential information. Trade secrets are defined by statute, including the federal Economic Espionage Act of 1996 (EEA) and state-level civil and criminal laws in the United States, many of which are modeled on the Uniform Trade Secrets Act. The EEA, for instance, defines trade secrets to include all types of financial, business, technical, economic, or engineering information, provided it derives economic value from not being generally known, and the owner has taken reasonable measures to keep it secret. Trade secret definitions are subject to court interpretation, which varies from state to state and across federal and state-level civil and criminal statutes.

Trade secret rights are rights to legal recourse to stop someone from using information without permission and to be compensated for any unauthorized use. As discussed in chapter 1, these rights are only available if your company (the information owner) has taken reasonable measures to protect it as confidential. If you and everyone else with access consistently protects confidential information, you establish your company's legal rights to it. The information becomes a trade secret in part through the collective effort of protecting it. Only through these cooperative and consistent efforts can your company establish legal rights to stop unauthorized use and to recover any damages that result from trade secret theft or unconsented use.

If you don't treat information as confidential and your company has no legal rights to it, the information is fair game for anyone interested. Competitors can use it to beat your company in the market. Reporters can use it to publish articles that denigrate your company or reveal plans and strategies that embarrass your company. Customers will lose trust in your company and its ability to remain viable and to protect their sensitive or private information.

Unfortunately, your company will not know if its valuable confidential information qualifies as a trade secret unless and until your company is involved in trade secret litigation. Your firm's information must be misappropriated or stolen, and a judge or jury must render an official decision before you can know for sure if specific information is a trade secret. By then, it's too late because your company will have suffered a significant loss. In the meantime, the best thing you and your work colleagues can do to ensure that your company has trade secret rights is to protect confidential information with reasonable measures.

Choices and Implications

Your company has a lot of choice about what it protects as confidential. Applying the broad definition in the EEA, for example, almost any business information that your company owns and protects as confidential may qualify as a trade secret. The following cases offer examples of confidential information that has been claimed in litigation as trade secret:

- Bimbo Bakeries' recipe and manufacturing process that give Thomas' English muffins their "nooks and crannies," which were known by a company executive who accepted a comparable position with rival Hostess

- The Cleveland Clinic's vials of fluid that thieves purloined and replaced with similar vials containing tap water

- Cisco's programming source code for a security technology that was found on a former employee's computer at his start-up business, which was based on the stolen code

- American Airlines spill tables for the yield management system, an intricate system that airlines use to establish fares based on pricing strategies and flight schedules

- Eastman Kodak and 3M's design of a multimillion-dollar machine involved in the manufacturing of consumer photographic film, described in thousands of pages of hard copy documents

- Archer Daniels Midland's enzyme that gave farm-raised trout and salmon a pinkish hue similar to that of wild fish, which was at the center of a $300 million-dollar civil lawsuit

These cases provide a glimpse at the scope and diversity of trade secret treasures, all of which were confidential information prior to any trade secrets lawsuit. Your company could choose to protect as confidential all the information that is not required by law to be released, or it could choose not to protect any of its business information. Some companies choose to protect only their most sensitive information, their "crown jewels." Others choose to protect everything that is not officially released to the public. And many companies choose something in between.

The implications of these choices are significant. Those who protect only their most sensitive information have the benefit of focusing their security resources on the company's most valuable secrets. The downside is that everything else will likely be available to be used against the company by competitors and other profiteers.

Those who protect everything that is not officially released have the benefit of maintaining some control over the bits and pieces of information that can be aggregated to reveal the organization's strategies and tactics. The downside of this approach is that these organizations often struggle with the time, attention, and financial costs of protecting the vast amounts of information that are exchanged with frequency and in diverse circumstances.

Do you know what choices your company has made? Do you know what information owned by your company is regarded as confidential? If not, you should ask. Neither you nor your company gain if you protect information that is not confidential. Not only do such efforts waste resources, they cause confusion, which can undermine confidentiality potency. A positively confidential safe haven is created in part by clearly identifying the information worthy of protection.

Your company may use a term other than "confidential" to describe the body of information it has an interest in protecting. Some companies successfully classify their confidential information using terminology such as proprietary, secret, or classified. In such cases, the distinction between proprietary information (owned), confidential information (protected), and trade secrets (determined by a court)—however named by your company—still applies.

Private and Personal Information

Private information is also a subset of confidential information. While your company has complete choice about which business information it considers confidential, it has no choice about which personal information it must treat as private. The European Union Data Protection Directive, the Personal Information Protection and Electronic Data Act (Canada), the Personal Information Protection Law (Japan), the Privacy Act (Australia and New Zealand), the Information Technology Act (India), and other similar laws enacted by countries around the globe require that private information be protected. In the United States, federal regulations such as the Health Insurance Portability and Accountability Act of 1996 (HIPAA) and the Gramm-Leach-Bliley Financial Services Modernization Act of 1999 (GLB) impose obligations on companies to protect certain private information. Many state laws have similar requirements.

While the definitions in these statutes differ, private information can be generally defined as information that identifies a person, directly or indirectly, by reference to an identification number or by one or more factors specific to physical, physiological, mental, economic, cultural, or social identity. This information is also referred to as personally identifiable information (PII) and includes the name, age, income, sexual orientation, medical information, credit history, financial account information, and family records of employees and customers. Appendix A includes examples of private information. You should use it as a reference only if your company does not have its own list based on applicable regulations and its own policies.

Beware of Inconsistency

Identifying information as confidential or private will be an effective first step in protecting it only if everyone with access to it recognizes that the information is confidential and treats it accordingly. Conversely, inconsistency can destroy all the benefits of identifying information as confidential.

A tire manufacturer learned this lesson the hard way. The company had two divisions: one for car tires and one for truck tires. The car tire division's established policy was to protect car tire specifications as confidential. No similar policy existed in the truck tire division. The car tire division clearly marked its tire specifications as confidential while the truck tire division did not. Both divisions provided their product specifications to the same customer, a car and truck manufacturer.

The customer's procurement manager was confused. How could one set of tire specifications be confidential if the other set from the same company was not? The procurement manager gave both sets of specifications to a competing tire vendor in order to get another bid on both tire types. When the tire company learned of it, they claimed the car and truck manufacturer violated its confidentiality obligations to the tire manufacturer. The parties went to arbitration where the customer argued successfully that it had no confidentiality obligation with respect to either tire specifications because only one set had been marked confidential.

The tire manufacturer's inconsistent confidentiality designation on its two divisions' tire specifications weakened its confidentiality stance with its customer and in arbitration. In the tire manufacturer's case, it took an inconsistency stretching across two divisions to weaken the confidential status of its car tire specifications. Yet it doesn't take such a sweeping inconsistency involving many people and multiple operations to dilute a confidentiality designation. An inconsistency might involve one person who applies her own view, which differs from the departmental or organizational view, as to what is confidential or not. Even an isolated inconsistency will offset confidentiality identification. All it takes is one person who shares information without restriction to transform a clear secret into something only potentially confidential and ultimately widely known news.

Consider a case involving a client company that spent hundreds of thousands of dollars on security for a technical breakthrough that was going to be incorporated into a new product line. The company's spectacular growth required that it expand its operations into a new building, in part to isolate the development team and ensure the project's security. Soon after the decision was made to move into the new building, due to the project's success, a project summary appeared on the local business newspaper's front page. Someone in the facilities department was not aware of the project's sensitivity, so he included a brief description of it in the building permit for the new facility. A business journalist on the lookout for news she could glean from building permit applications stumbled upon it and ran with the story. All it took was one person's failure to recognize the information's confidentiality or, in this case, perhaps a failure to recognize that revealing information through the building permit process put it in jeopardy. A well-kept secret became headline news overnight. With bloggers and vloggers (video bloggers) focused on corporate activities, this type of leak is becoming more common. It can take only a few hours before the whole world knows everything about a sensitive project or technical breakthrough once it is exposed online. If the information is identified as confidential to everyone with access to it, it is more likely to be protected against such indiscretions.

The Inventory Paradox

It is good business practice for your company to provide you with a list of the information it deems confidential. Without a list of examples, it is hard to know which information your company has chosen to hold secret. While a quality assurance engineer may believe that the test equipment he helped to develop is obviously confidential, it might not be obvious to someone in the marketing department.

Just as we have different opinions about the confidentiality of our salaries and our diet, we can also have different opinions about the confidentiality of the business information that we handle at work. After all, the diversity of cultures, backgrounds, viewpoints, work experiences, and professional interests represented in any organization will impact how individuals think about confidentiality and privacy.

The work environment itself may make it difficult for some to recognize confidential information. Many lose their perspective when they work with certain information day in and day out. Information recognized as confidential initially may become so familiar that those working with it think of it as commonplace and forget it is unique and valuable to their company.

Competing interests can also pull at us in ways that diminish our sense of what is confidential. We want to be helpful, provide good service, and appear knowledgeable. Information may seem less confidential when someone we want to impress is asking for or about it.

These are some of the practical reasons why you should be clear and specific about what information your company considers confidential. There are compelling legal reasons as well. In the seminal case of *Motorola, Inc. v. Fairchild Camera and Instrument Corporation, Inc. (366 F. Supp. 1173 (1973))*, Motorola brought an action against its former employees who had resigned their engineering positions with Motorola to work for Fairchild, a competitor. Each of the offending engineers had signed an agreement with Motorola promising to

> ... maintain strictly confidential ... all data and information of the company which I may originate or of which I learn during my employment with the company and which is of a confidential or secret nature such as product, machine, and process developments, whether patentable or not patentable, manufacturing "know-how" and specifications, cost and pricing practices, customers' lists, records of customers' requirements and usages, personnel records, company financial records and the like; and upon termination of my employment with the company for any reason whatsoever, I will not take with me or remove documentary material of the company on such data and information, or any record or copy thereof.

In 1973, the United States District Court for the District of Arizona held that, while the offending employees signed nondisclosure agreements (NDAs) that prohibited them from taking confidential materials with them when they left Motorola, the agreements were not enforceable because Motorola failed to provide a list or inventory detailing the specific types of information the employees should keep confidential. Despite the description and examples of confidential information included in the NDA itself, the court concluded that

The evidence established there was no list or index of any kind in existence in Motorola's records … as to what plaintiff considered to be a proprietary trade secret. The evidence also established that in other similar companies … such restrictive agreements were implemented by furnishing the employee a list of employer-claimed secrets at the time of employment; during employment as additions or deletions were made; and at termination by requiring a signed document acknowledging specifically identified and claimed trade secrets.

In effect, the court said an NDA can be enforced only if the party wanting to enforce it has made clear which specific information is confidential. In the case of *Motorola vs. Fairchild*, the NDA was not enforceable. Think about all of the NDAs that your company relies on to help ensure that those with access to its confidential information protect it. These NDAs may serve their purpose only if the information they purport to protect is specified with more detail than is typically found in an NDA.

Some trade secret experts believe there is another legal reason for identifying an organization's confidential information. Under the Sarbanes-Oxley Public Company Accounting Reform and Investor Protection Act of 2002 (SOX), standards for all public boards, management, and public accounting firms in the United States were established to strengthen corporate accounting controls. Public companies are now obligated to identify and value their financial assets. Many trade secret experts interpret financial assets to include intellectual assets (confidential information and intellectual property). These experts conclude then that SOX mandates confidential information identification and valuation.

Despite these practical and legal reasons for your company to have a list of the information it wants to protect as confidential, it is unlikely that you have such a list that is complete and up-to-date. Maintaining a current inventory of dynamic confidential information is challenging. What is confidential depends largely on timing, context, level of detail, and aggregation. Information—and its confidentiality—is a moving target. Its sensitivity may change as new concepts emerge and your company develops and launches products. When a new product strategy is in its early development stages, it is very sensitive and should be classified as confidential. Once the strategy is implemented, information about it may be considered nonconfidential. Time-sensitive information is reclassified or declassified when the sensitivity changes. This is easy to do, particularly when there is a public announcement unveiling the previously secret information. Still, employees will need to stay tuned in, so they continue treating confidential information as confidential, even when there is internal buzz about the deal, product, restructuring, or posturing. Lively internal discussions are quite different from a public announcement. One is cause for concern and requires more vigilant efforts to protect the information. The other is cause for untying restraints, particularly if the announcement unveils good news.

The context and degree of detail can also affect information's sensitivity. A full copy of your company's operating policies and procedures might be confidential. A brief summary of them, used to illustrate your company's corporate leadership, might be nonconfidential. Similarly, a compilation of detailed information may have a different level of sensitivity than individual data. For example, particular customer names may not be confidential. Your company might refer to them on a customer list to establish credibility in promotional literature. Your company's detailed customer database or data warehouse, however, which contains a compilation of customer preferences, purchases, budgets, and credit reports, would be confidential.

In contrast, individual data may be more sensitive than aggregated information. Individual employee data such as salary and merit increases over an employee's tenure with her employer is likely confidential. A compilation of employee data such as salaries and merit increases for all employees, without employee names, may be nonconfidential.

Confidential information may take many forms and may be embedded in a variety of media. It can be revealed through your conversations, voicemail messages, calendar entries, paper documents, videos, e-mail messages, blog posts, texts, instant messages, tweets, and other electronic communications. All forms of confidential information inherit the same classification.

Identifying confidential information is a dynamic process. You are ultimately responsible for using informed good judgment, actively and dynamically, to understand which of your company's information is confidential and thus needs your protection. Knowing what is confidential can become easy, but it does require a conscious effort. Your company's definition of confidential information and its list of examples or the list in appendix A should help.

Your biggest challenge will likely be to keep these references in mind when you need to quickly make decisions about how to respond to an inquiry, request, or statement. A posting that just made its way to your computer or personal digital assistant (PDA) screen via an RSS feed (a Web-based tool that checks the user's subscribed feeds for new content and then downloads updates) may trigger you to reply, or you may be tempted to answer a question posed by someone calling on the telephone or stopping you in the exhibit hall of a technical conference. The following questions should supply brain Velcro, something to stick in your mind when you are lulled or pulled into thinking confidential information is not:

- **Potentially damaging?** Might the information you are tempted to share provide a competitive advantage or be damaging if disclosed without restriction?
- **Useful to a competitor?** Would a competitor's intelligence professional or an industry journalist want this information?

If the answer to either of these questions is yes, the information is probably confidential. If you are uncertain in a particular situation whether releasing specific information might be injurious, ask your manager or a member of your organization's legal department for help to get clarity. Until then, it is generally best for your company *and* you if you assume that information is confidential and should be revealed with caution and only by those who know when, where, and to whom it is most appropriate to share.

Chapter 3 Spot Quiz
Identify the Information You Need to Protect

(The answer key can be found in appendix D)

Which of the following statements illustrate a lack of understanding about identifying confidential information?

A. Not only is personal or private information subject to company-imposed controls, it is also government-regulated at multiple levels, including state, federal, and international.

B. Within your company, a compilation of individual pieces of information may have a different classification than any particular individual piece of that information.

C. Information that is considered confidential in one division of your company does not need to be treated as confidential in other divisions.

D. You must not rely solely on any inventory of classified information. Such inventories may be outdated or incomplete. You must supplement confidential information examples with both your own informed good judgment and the advice of appropriate authorities within your company, especially when evaluating information that is either not included or for which the classification may have changed.

Is the following statement true or false?

All of your company's confidential information is proprietary, but not all of its proprietary information is confidential.

Make It Clear
That Confidential Information
Is Indeed Confidential

CHAPTER 4

Chapter 4 Takeaways

How do you make it clear that confidential information is confidential?

- Require a nondisclosure agreement (NDA) to create a relationship of trust.
- Indicate information's confidentiality conspicuously.
- Use confidentiality classifications that identify the owner.

NDAs, the Next Best Thing to Pillow Talk

In a typical marriage, there's an agreement, often explicit, to create a relationship where confidentiality is respected and maintained. "Pillow talk" is the shorthand phrase some people use to refer to the agreement that anything shared never goes further than the bedroom. "I've got some pillow talk," you might say before letting your wife know that your friend confided in you that he is taking early retirement. The reference to "pillow talk," or asking your spouse to keep your news between the two of you, informs your spouse that what you are about to say is confidential. There is a mutual understanding that the consequences of either partner revealing the other's secrets would tear at the fabric of their trust. These consequences reinforce the agreement of confidentiality, in part because the collateral for maintaining that trust may be the marriage itself.

In the business world, our secrets aren't nearly as safe. We often need to share confidential information with people we do not know well or at all. We may like and respect a prospective customer, contractor, business partner, supplier, or student intern, but without a formal agreement, we have no basis to trust that if we say something is confidential, it will be held as our spouse holds our pillow talk.

A nondisclosure or confidentiality agreement, often referred to as an NDA, establishes a relationship where confidentiality can be enforced between strangers and between organizations that are constantly changing. An NDA binds the parties to the agreement to hold certain information as confidential. This is especially important in business where most people who need a company's confidential information have an interest in using it for their own benefit, which conflicts with the company owner's interests.

If there is no NDA between your company and a prospective customer, for example, you can't expect that the prospect will keep secret your plans for a future product. Your prospect, like the car and truck manufacturer in chapter 3, has an interest in sharing those plans with your competitors. By doing so, your prospect can find out if your competition is planning to develop a similar product and at what price. By sharing information about your new product, your prospective customer can create competition that drives down your product's price. You can tell the prospect that your new unreleased product plans are confidential. You can mark every document that you deliver as "confidential." But without establishing a legally binding confidentiality agreement, your confidentiality declarations may be meaningless.

An NDA establishes a binding legal relationship in which confidentiality is enforceable—in court if necessary. An NDA also provides evidence, which your company may need in a future trade secrets lawsuit, that you took steps to ensure that the people with whom you share information will use it only to benefit your company.

Without an NDA, your disclosure to a prospect, customer, supplier, temporary employee, or colleague may render the information nonconfidential, no matter how vehemently and clearly you declare that it is confidential. If the person to whom you reveal information has not agreed to a legally binding confidentiality relationship with your company, he is not obligated to protect the company information you disclose. Agreeing to the terms of an NDA invokes responsibilities, while avoiding an NDA frees the avoider from NDA obligations.

The Social Network movie about Facebook founder Mark Zuckerberg may give you a different impression. Cameron and Tyler Winklevoss and their business partner Divya Narendra hired fellow Harvard University undergraduate Zuckerberg to program their Web site, Harvard Connection. In the movie, Zuckerberg does not sign an NDA or other formal agreement with the Winklevoss twins, Narendra, or Harvard Connection. In fact, the Zuckerberg portrayed in the film might have refused to sign a Harvard Connection NDA to maintain his freedom from its obligations. The movie shows neither the Winklevoss twins nor Narendra taking any steps to protect their ideas about Harvard Connection. Yet the Winklevoss twins negotiated a $65 million settlement in 2009, which they filed suit to increase in late 2010, in part based on their claim that Zuckerberg stole Harvard Connection ideas to create Facebook. While the public may never know the true story of how the Winklevoss twins were able to win their settlement, we can assume that some implied agreement, such as one presumed between company founders, to protect Harvard

Connection confidential information was the basis of the trade secret claim (which was only one of the Winklevoss twins' many claims against Zuckerberg).

NDAs, express or implied, can protect multibillion-dollar ideas, and they can also create multimillion-dollar liabilities. For many companies, the potential liability is not worth taking a risk on a new idea. For example, let's imagine that you conceive an exciting new board game and you want to present the idea to Mattel, Hasbro, Parker Brothers, or Electronic Arts. They will not want to sign an NDA because they will not want to establish a legally binding confidentiality relationship that obligates them to protect your idea. If there is a confidentiality relationship and some information that you make known shows up in one of their products, there would be consequences for the game company. They might have to pay you royalties, or you might be able to prevent them from selling their products that incorporate your ideas. To avoid these consequences, leading companies from almost every industry will delay for as long as possible signing an NDA with you if your purpose is to obligate them to protect your ideas as your own. In fact, they may have you sign an agreement that you will *not* reveal confidential information to them as you, a nonemployee, present your proposal for their new products.

In a marriage, a relationship of confidentiality can often be established without a formal agreement, although an informal agreement to honor pillow talk is not a substitute for an NDA. If one spouse needs to make known confidential employer information to the other spouse, it may be appropriate for the spouse receiving the information to sign an NDA to protect company-owned business information.

In business, an NDA, or an agreement with similar confidentiality commitments, articulates in a legally binding document the promise to keep confidential information confidential and carries consequences if the agreement is breached. The NDA is required to establish trust. In marriage, trust comes because the consequences of violating it can be as disastrous as divorce. In business, trust comes because violating an NDA is a breach of contract, with consequences that may include an expensive and acrimonious lawsuit, such as the one portrayed in *The Social Network*. In both cases, what you are trusting is that, when you declare that something is confidential, it will be recognized as such. If it is not, an NDA allows your company to enforce its rights against the person or organization that broke its confidentiality promise.

Working with Someone Who Will Not Sign an NDA

People or companies to whom you want to disclose confidential information may refuse to sign an NDA. Venture capitalists are well-known to rebuff requests to enter into NDAs and may consider you naïve if you ask them to sign one. Prospective customers and business partners may also refuse to sign any agreements requiring them to maintain secrecy. There are instances when it may be worthwhile to proceed with divulging confidential information without an NDA.

What can you do when you think that the potential benefits of revealing confidential information outweigh the potential detriment of doing so without an NDA? If you have the authority to make the judgment call to disclose information despite the recipient's refusal to sign an NDA, then immediately after you make known confidential information, you can send a written notification that your company considers the information confidential. I helped one of my clients develop the following letter to use when disclosing pre-release product information to a prospect who refuses to sign an NDA:

Dear _____,

I appreciate your time in our meeting today. I understand that you are not willing to sign our nondisclosure agreement. I expressed to you that the information I shared about _____ is confidential. I believe that we have a "gentlemen's agreement" that you will not reveal this information to our competitors. I want to acknowledge in writing that I appreciate your understanding that this information is very sensitive and valuable to our company and it would be quite damaging to us if you were to share it with our competitors or any other third parties.

Best, _____

While no legally binding confidentiality relationship is established, this note helps to deter prospects from sharing information with the company's competitors. A handshake or gentleman's agreement reinforced by a thank-you note is not a substitute for an NDA. Rather, it is an attempt to create a relationship of trust based on hope, guilt, or a personal connection. It is better than nothing. But it is far more effective to have an enforceable contract established through an NDA whenever possible. An NDA infuses meaning into a declaration that something is confidential. It means there may be consequences if the signer of the NDA does not maintain the information's secrecy.

Declare Information Confidential

As discussed in chapter 3, the determination of which information is confidential, aside from private information, which is defined and governed by laws and regulations, is ultimately a matter of the owner's choice. Others are made aware of that choice when you and everyone else who handles the information declares and treats it as confidential.

The NDA establishes a relationship of trust that is a container for sharing sensitive information. Once that safe container is established, you still need to make sure that anyone with whom you share confidential information clearly understands what is confidential. Any uncertainty may circumvent the NDA's coverage.

In your personal life, if you want last night's raucus dinner party to be forgotten, you need to tell your confidant what specifically should be kept secret. Otherwise, though you may have established a safe container of trust with your friend, she may use the information to make interesting conversation with her friends and family or talk to you about the evening's excesses while at her hair salon where others may overhear names and tidbits of the conversation. By telling your trusted friend that you want information about last night's dinner party to be kept confidential, you distinguish it from the information that you share without reservation.

Similarly, if your company chooses to hold its product plans and manufacturing processes secret, every person with access to the plans and processes will need to be notified, or the recipients may use the information to make interesting conversation with colleagues employed by competitors or the press.

A confidential information inventory is a useful reference that lets you know the categories of information your company considers confidential (see appendix A). If you develop a budget for a new project, you might check your company's inventory to see if budgets and, more specifically, project budgets are listed. If your company hasn't distributed a list of examples of its confidential information, someone has probably informed you in some other way, perhaps in your new hire orientation or some subesquent training, about what categories of information are company confidential. Alternately, your company may rely on policy documents that define confidential information and list examples.

If you are an information originator, it is probably your responsibility, perhaps with your manager's oversight, to apply your company's definition of confidential information, refer to the list of examples in the inventory (if one is available), and determine if the information you develop is confidential. If it is your responsibility to determine whether information is confidential, you must also make your decision clear to others who have access to the information. Whether in the form of an electronic file, a paper document, a video clip, a verbal comment, an entry in a calendar or task list, an e-mail, or an instant message, others can understand that information is confidential only if you let them know that it is.

The NDAs signed by your colleagues, contractors, and suppliers probably do not state which information is confidential with more specificity than, for example, the Motorola NDA discussed in chapter 3. It is not reasonable to expect that those who may have access to your organization's information will intuitively know what is confidential. You also can't expect that they will refer to an inventory, review information protection policy documents, or take the initiative to treat something as secret if the information is provided to them without an indication that it is confidential.

The Confidentiality Notice

A confidentiality notice is a declaration that specific information—in whatever form it is in—is indeed confidential. It states an expectation that certain information must be treated as secret. It is the signal you give to those with whom you have established a relationship of trust (for example, via an NDA) that this particular information is subject to that trust and the NDA. The confidentiality notice is the critical link between determining which information is confidential (chapter 3) and causing others to protect it.

When I am called upon as an expert witness in a trade secret lawsuit, the primary question I am asked to opine on is, "Did the party claiming theft of trade secrets apply reasonable efforts to protect them?" As discussed in chapter 1, a company must demonstrate that it applied reasonable efforts to protect information in order to establish it as a trade secret. In many trade secrets cases, the alleged trade secrets are embodied in hard copy documents and electronic files, which the defendant is alleged to have stolen or misappropriated. If the documents or files are not marked "confidential" or similarly tagged with proprietary, secret, or internal use, it may indicate that the company did not consider the documents or files to contain trade secrets.

If the document or file does have a notification indicating confidentiality, a threshold of establishing trade secrets is crossed. Although the label does not, in itself, determine trade secret status, it provides a visible cue of confidentiality for anyone who sees the document or file, whether employee, business partner, judge, or jury. Making it clear that information in written, electronic, or verbal form is confidential not only notifies the recipient that the information is confidential and identifies its owner, but it will also be a critical factor in determining whether your company has taken reasonable measures to protect that information and thereby establish it as a trade secret.

Information Classifications

Information classification is a kind of shorthand that answers three questions:

- Is it confidential?
- Whose information is it?
- What kind of protection should I apply?

All confidentiality notices should answer these three basic questions. While a simple confidentiality notice, such as the word "confidential" in the footer of a document, may be sufficient to put others on notice that someone considers the information secret, it does not indicate who owns the information. It should. How else will you let your company's customers, contractors, suppliers, temporary workers, and others know that it is your company that is declaring the information confidential? Forget your company's name in the confidentiality notice, and a customer might assume that the proposal you sent to her marked "confidential" is *her* confidential information. A contractor might assume that his market findings report, which you mark "confidential," is *his* confidential information. You avoid this potential confusion by including your company's name next to the word "confidential."

Information classifications can go one step further. They can be a shorthand declaration that your company owns the information, which is confidential, and that it should be protected in a particular way.

After decades of helping hundreds of leading companies in diverse industries establish information classifications, I have found the schema diagrammed in the following figure and described in the subsequent table to be a best practice for confidential information classification.

Information Classification Best Practices

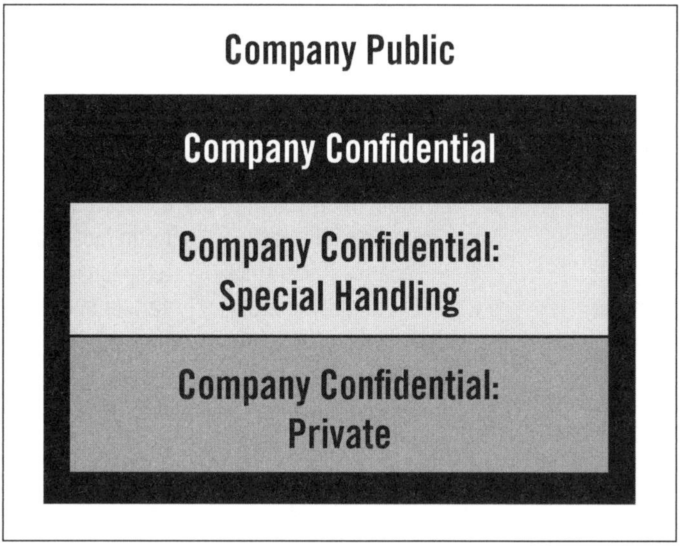

Company Public

Company Confidential

Company Confidential: Special Handling

Company Confidential: Private

Figure 4

Confidential Information Classifications		
Classification	Definition	Examples
Company Confidential	Any information that might provide a competitive advantage or could cause business harm or legal exposure if the information is used or disclosed without restriction	Product plans, manufacturing processes, test methods, sales projections, and employee lists
Company Confidential: Special Handling	A subset of Company Confidential information, typically extremely sensitive business or technical information, that requires additional measures to guard against unauthorized use or disclosure to avoid significant business harm or legal exposure	Business plans, acquisition strategies, and software source code
Company Confidential: Private	Nonpublic, personally identifiable information requiring special treatment because it identifies a person, directly or indirectly, by reference to an identification number or by one or more factors specific to physical, physiological, mental, economic, cultural or social identity	An individual's name connected with age, birthplace, address, telephone number, credit card or account information, purchase or credit history, and medical records

Table 3

The above classification schema works well for most companies for several reasons:

- It makes clear that information labeled with any of the three confidentiality classifications is confidential information owned by the company, assuming the company uses its name instead of the word "Company" in the above example.

- The modifiers "Special Handling" and "Private," which distinguish these classifications, can be intuitively understood. While some individuals may not know the exact implications of the "Private" designation, most will assume that the information should be treated with some kind of privacy controls, such as those imposed by government regulations. Similarly, while some individuals may not know how "Special Handling" information is to be handled, the term can be intuitively understood as meaning that there are unique safeguards that should be applied to it. A classification schema that is easily understood can do the heavy lifting of notifying anyone with access to the classified information that it is confidential, owned by the named company, and should be treated in a particular way.

You do not need to advocate for changing your company's information classifications so they mirror the ones described here. If your company uses different classification categories that work well, changing them may cause an unnecessary diversion. The clear, intuitive classifications just described provide a taxonomy that is useful in implementing a cost-effective information protection strategy for many companies, but it may not be the right solution for your company. I have helped hundreds of companies develop and implement information classification strategies that work well for them, though they do not exactly immitate the best practice classification categories.

Information classifications are a protection tool. They do not, by themselves, protect information. People and technology do. If the tool is like a hammer, simple and easy to use, it will be used. If it is complicated and difficult to use, like expanded features on a remote control, it is less likely to be understood and used and thus less likely to encourage confidentiality protection. More important than the specific classification wordings, definitions, or levels is that your company's confidentiality notices include your company's name and an indication of how the information should be treated.

One purpose of classifications is to help corporate functions set protection levels that correspond to information sensitivity levels and types. Requirements for each confidential information level can be assigned in information protection policies, NDAs, communication for education and awareness, and an information technology (IT) security infrastructure.

Your company's IT department, for example, may need a classification system to properly protect the integrity, privacy, and confidentiality of content, files, metadata, and data aggregations. Many IT departments invest in technology to monitor highly sensitive information transmissions over the company's network. They can limit the administrative investment in monitoring tools by applying them only to data classified as "Special Handling."

Similarly, your company's legal department may need a classification system to ensure that it protects intellectual property rights, meets contractual obligations, and avoids misappropriation. The "Special Handling" classification applied to certain highly sensitive third-party information entrusted to your company can help accomplish these goals.

While IT, legal, and other corporate functions provide essential business processes and technology safeguards, you, other employees, and outside stakeholders simply need to know if the information you access is confidential and, if so, whether there is any special treatment that you should apply to it. A good information classification notice answers these questions with elegant simplicity.

Getting Practical: Labeling Documents and Files

I have described how you make clear that something is confidential by first creating a relationship of trust and then declaring that the confidential information is confidential. Classifications can be used as a declaration of confidentiality, ownership, and protection level. Controls and protection measures appropriate to each of the classifications are described in chapter 8 (see tables 7 and 9).

Here we address the practical issue of how to give notice of confidentiality using a classification. The best approach often depends on the type of material that embodies the information. You are probably already familiar with using a confidentiality notice on some documents. Perhaps you have put the word "confidential" in the footer of a spreadsheet or placed the word "secret" in the watermark of a draft proposal. You have also probably seen confidentiality notices, legends, and markings on a variety of documents you have received, including e-mails. To declare information confidential, it should be labeled as such in all its representations. Attributes of an effective confidentiality notice include that it

- Is conspicuous (attracts attention)
- Conveys a confidentiality classification
- Declares ownership

The notice may be a footer at the bottom of a document, a splash screen that precedes authorized access to a database, a description of restrictions on permitted uses of a lecture that consititutes the first slide of a PowerPoint® presentation, or a sentence or two introducing participants to a live discussion that informs them that it is confidential.

In my consulting work, companies often ask for guidance on the form and content of confidentiality notices, and they frequently have the same concerns:

- Should confidentiality notices be on the footer of every page, or is it sufficient for a notice to be on the cover page?
- Should confidentiality notices be in bold type?
- Is it preferable to show a confidentiality notice as a watermark on a printout?
- What color should the confidentiality notice be?

If your company's policies do not specifically answer these questions, you can follow the simple guidelines presented here. The purpose of a confidentiality notice is to inform anyone who accesses the information that it is confidential. You can do this most effectively by making sure that the notice is conspicuous and legible (or audible). If your PowerPoint presentation template uses only twenty-four-point typeface or larger, it may not be appropriate to have a confidentiality notice in less than fourteen-point type. If the entries in your Excel® spreadsheet are all in ten-point type, it may be suitable for the confidentiality notice to also be in ten-point type. Using watermarks, colorful type, marked file folders, or other means to make confidentiality notices more conspicuous adds to their effectiveness.

Confidentiality notices can and should be adapted to suit particular applications. For example, if you are developing a request for a proposal (RFP), it should be marked with the classification of its most sensitive information, perhaps "Company Confidential: Special Handling." This marking can be in the header or footer of every page or every other page, on the cover, or in a watermark. What is important is that it is easily visible to anyone who receives the document or file.

In addition to the classification label, it is often useful to add instructions, such as

- Copying of this RFP, in any medium, in whole or in part, or disclosure of its contents to anyone other than the authorized recipient is strictly prohibited.
- Do not discuss the contents of this document without the originator's permission.

Such add-ons are limitless. In the case of your RFP, you might include a paragraph with the following statement:

This RFP is confidential and should not be shared with any third party. It should be stored on the recipient's computing system(s) in encrypted form. If the recipient's proposal is not accepted, this RFP and recipient's response to it must be destroyed.

Appendix B, "Sample Confidentiality Notices," provides several examples of instructions you can use to augment the confidentiality classifications in your documents, assuming your company permits you to do so. If so, you can be creative in including as much instruction as is appropriate for the sensitivity of the information and the medium in which it is embodied.

Label What You Bring to Life

You may be shaking your head and thinking, "Okay, this is a good idea, but I'm staring at several file cabinets, all crammed tight with documents. Beyond that wall and in the building across the parking lot, there are more. Likewise in my computer and servers on the company's network, there are millions of files that should be marked as 'confidential'. It would be an impossible task to access them all, determine their classification one by one, and label them."

Generally speaking, you would be right. Technology that can find, classify, and label confidential information exists, but investing in it is a corporate decision. How do other well-intentioned busy people faced with a similar conundrum handle it? They look forward, not back. In other words, only when you use or distribute a confidential file or document do you need to mark it with the proper classification, such as "(Your Company's Name) Confidential." Consider the old files stored in filing cabinets and hard drives dead. Using or distributing a document or file brings it back to life. When you open an old draft of a document and use it as a template for a new one, for example, or when you prepare to send to a contractor a file that you haven't accessed in years, it is time to mark it with the appropriate confidentiality notification if one is not included.

You can also notify others that whole repositories of dead information are confidential. For example, you might lock the file cabinets and place signs on them, encrypt the hard drives that contain confidential information, and include a logon screen to the hard drives to notify users that the information repository contains confidential information:

> This device (or cabinet as the case may be) may contain confidential information.
> As you use specific files, mark them with the appropriate classification.

Confidentiality notices on repositories of confidential information can, however, be dangerous if they provide thieves with a pointer to where your most valuable information is stored. Some argue that, by marking things as confidential, you not only tell the good guys what you own and expect them to keep secret, you also put thieves on notice as to where to find things they may want to steal.

If you can keep information secret without relying on others to do the same, you do not need to mark it confidential. For example, you may have a file cabinet full of confidential documents that you keep in your office. If you always lock the cabinet when you are away and you have the only key, you probably do not need to and, in fact, should not post a sign over it stating, "This cabinet contains confidential information." There is no reason to have a warning sign if it only creates temptation.

Similarly, if you keep your team meeting notes in a file on your laptop, encrypt the file, never let the laptop out of your sight, and never share the document with anyone, you probably don't need to mark it as "confidential." Only when others may see the confidential meeting notes do you need to include a confidentiality notice, though it is a good habit to mark all confidential material with the appropriate classification when you create it so no confidential information that may eventually be seen by others goes unlabeled.

Classification notices should be part of a protection arsenal or precautionary force field (see chapter 8). If you lock all your doors, put a security alarm on your home, and place a sign on your lawn indicating a security alarm protects it, it is not an invitation to steal from your home. Instead, it is a deterrent. The classification notice should similarly convey that you and your company take protecting valuable information seriously.

The Danger of Overusing or Misusing the Confidential Label

Some individuals insist that, rather than take the time to distinguish confidential from nonconfidential information, it is a lot easier to simply classify everything as confidential. The problem with this approach is that not everything *is* confidential. An invitation to your company's holiday party, the company's public job posting for a procurement specialist, and the marketing materials on your company's Web site are examples of nonconfidential information. Treating everything as confidential is confounding. Making a clear distinction between confidential and nonconfidential information is essential to avoiding confusion and taking the initial step toward protection.

Many people use an automatically generated footer for all their e-mail messages. The footer states that the contents of the e-mail are confidential. But if that footer appears at the end of an automatic reply message when you are on vacation as well as on a highly sensitive statement of concern, for example, "If we cannot pass the quality test by Friday, we will lose our contract with XYZ Company," a recipient will not know that one is confidential and the other is not. Including the confidentiality statement in both types of e-mail is not helping to clarify what is confidential. In fact, it is harmful. Overusing confidentiality notices can diminish and ultimately negate their value.

I mentioned earlier in this chapter that I am often called upon as a litigation consultant and an expert witness to help determine if a company took reasonable measures to protect its secrets. Two questions I ask as I review documents associated with a case are

- Was the confidential information marked as "confidential"?
- Was the nonconfidential information also marked as "confidential"?

If the latter is true, the company has probably failed to distinguish, and put recipients on notice, that certain (but not all) information is company confidential. It can be as damaging to mark nonconfidential information as "confidential" as it is to not mark confidential information as such. In either case, confidential information is not clearly identified.

Verbal Notification of Confidentiality

Confidentiality can be conveyed very positively with the result that everyone listening feels privileged to receive the information. "What I'm about to discuss is highly confidential," you might say before you begin to reveal company secrets during a meeting. "If we can all keep what is said in this room confidential, we'll increase our chances of achieving our goals." The more you can reinforce your confidentiality message, the better.

If you write confidential information on a whiteboard during a meeting, you might note at the very top, "Keep this confidential," and then erase the information before you leave the meeting room. One clever company posts signs on all its conference room whiteboards that read, "Erase after use. Spies have booked this room after you."

You can also reinforce the confidentiality message by reminding participants as you end a meeting, "Before you go, please keep in mind that what you heard today is confidential." These clear and conspicuous verbal confidentiality notifications help ensure that meeting participants protect confidential information, although they may not be enough. Many NDAs require recipients of verbally disclosed information to treat it as confidential only if the person disclosing the information provides written confirmation that the information is indeed confidential. In other words, when you disclose confidential information verbally, you may need to do more than state that it is confidential. The relationship of trust created by the NDA between your company and the person to whom you disclose confidential information may depend on you reinforcing that statement in writing after your verbal disclosure.

Are you familiar with the terms of the NDA signed by those to whom you reveal confidential information? They may require that you send a confidentiality acknowledgement in writing, typically within thirty days of disclosure, in order for the information you disclosed to be considered confidential.

When I have shared confidential information under these terms, such as when I demonstrated a pre-release software product to a prospective licensee, I have followed up with a written statement, which is typically a simple e-mail message:

> In your office on Thursday, September 22, 2011, I shared with you my proposal for a software product to be customized for your company. I stated to you at that time that my software and proposal for customizing it are confidential. Pursuant to the nondisclosure agreement between us, I am confirming that verbal confidentiality statement with this e-mail.

If I didn't send a written follow-up notice, the information I disclosed verbally would not be covered by the NDA. Yet, when I send such a written confidentiality confirmation after a verbal disclosure, the recipient typically tells me that I am one of the very few who has complied with this confidentiality confirmation requirement.

Many people who reveal confidential information verbally and do not acknowledge in writing that they did so are exposing the information to loss without NDA coverage. Think about the last time you shared confidential information with someone over the telephone or in a meeting. You may have let the person know that the information is confidential. Perhaps you even confirmed with him that he had signed an NDA. Unless you reviewed the terms of that agreement and followed its requirements, however, the confidential information you presented may not be protected.

Do Not Assume Something Is Confidential Just Because Someone Says It Is

For the same reasons a game development company may not want to be burdened with your confidential ideas for a new board game, your company's best interests may not be served by receiving confidential information from others. While asking for feedback on Twitter or on a corporate Facebook page, commonly called "crowdsourcing," may be a great way for your company to reach out to customers for their ideas, if handled improperly, it could lead to disaster. The relationship of trust created by an NDA carries responsibilities, as well as consequences for failure to meet them. It is in your company's best interest to take on this burden only when necessary. If you are working with a customer with whom your company has an NDA and the NDA obligates your company to protect customer confidential information, you will want to be careful to accept only the confidential information you need. Taking in more only adds to your own and your company's responsibilities.

You will also want to be careful to not acknowledge that something is confidential when it is not. The owner should not designate information as confidential if it is available without limit to others, such as on a public Web site. A vendor representative may tell you that his product's yield data is confidential, and he may mark a product yield report as "confidential" as a way of putting you on notice that he wants you to keep it secret. If you know the product yield report is available on an industry association Web site or if you have seen his company's product yield data presented at a technical conference, it is probably not confidential. But if you don't challenge the vendor's confidentiality designation, you and your company may be taking on an unwanted restriction and burden.

Whenever you receive allegedly confidential information, understand that this designation comes with a responsibility. Typically, it is subject to an NDA. If so, you and your company have an obligation to use it only for specific purposes and to protect it. Therefore, it's a good idea to challenge someone who indicates that something is confidential if you believe that it is not.

Reclassifying or Declassifying Information

Confidential information evolves and changes in an information ecosystem. As information advances, new details may increase the need for secrecy. As the ecosystem transforms, such as at the moment the company's annual report is released, the quarterly financials convert from highly confidential to publicly available. In some cases, there is a clear demarcation when something that was confidential becomes nonconfidential, such as when a new product, developed in stealth mode, is launched. In many other cases, it is not clear. Some information that was highly confidential in its inception stage may become less sensitive, but still confidential, when it is shared with supply chain partners, for example.

Both the initial classification and the reclassification of information—whether from confidential to nonconfidential or from one level of confidentiality to another—require that you consciously determine, and then declare a new classification. If you don't determine, and then declare a reclassification when appropriate, you run into the problem of overusing or misusing the confidential label, which diminishes or possibly cancels its value.

Reclassification and declassification is easier than it may sound. It just requires you to keep information's dynamic character in mind. Is it confidential? If so, declare it so with a confidentiality notification. If the information or circumstances surrounding the information change, be prepared to declassify or reclassify it. After that, declare that the change has been made by changing the confidentiality notification to reflect the new classification. Or declare that the information is no longer confidential by removing confidentiality notices from its embodiments. Just as many companies require that documents be marked with a confidentiality legend only when brought to life with use, many companies only require that you unmark or reclassify documents when you bring them to life with use. You may want to check your company's confidential information reclassification policy to determine your role in the process.

Confidentiality Notices for Work Areas

The observation of a research and development (R&D) project, a manufacturing facility, a prototype test lab, or other work area can reveal secrets. Situating facilities for this work apart from the rest of the corporate campus may help prevent outsiders from gaining access to company secrets. Physical security as well as digital security bolsters confidentiality declarations (see chapter 8). Just as marking a document or file as "confidential" can establish that it is subject to confidentiality restrictions, placing a sign on the door to a work area can have a similar effect. Many tools are available to give outsiders notice that information, including that which may be absorbed unintentionally, is confidential. A sign such as "Restricted Area: For R&D Employees Only" is one way to declare that the information within is confidential.

Your vigilance and creativity can make the difference between recognized and protected trade secrets and ordinary, ho-hum, commonplace information. Declaring — and reinforcing with confidentiality labels, signs, and statements — specific information as confidential is essential to producing the former. The first step is establishing a relationship of trust with an NDA or similar agreement. Then the benefits of that relationship can be realized when you make known which information is subject to the trusted parties' NDA protection responsibilities.

Chapter 4 Spot Quiz
Make It Clear That Confidential Information Is Indeed Confidential

(The answer key can be found in appendix D)

Based on current best practices, which of the following statements are true?

A. Sales projections, employee lists, and test methods are examples of information that might be classified as "Company Confidential."

B. Business plans, acquisition strategies, and source codes are examples of information that might be classified as "Company Confidential: Special Handling."

C. Records containing an individual's Social Security number, credit card and bank account information, or medical history are examples of information that might be classified as "Company Confidential: Private."

D. All of the above

Is the following statement true or false?

If a piece of information is clearly marked with its appropriate classification, such as Company Confidential, Company Confidential: Special Handling, or Company Confidential: Private, both in hard copy and in all its electronic forms, then you and your company have done everything that is needed to prove you have taken reasonable measures to protect it.

Determine Your Need to Reveal Before You Share Confidential Information

CHAPTER 5

Chapter 5 Takeaways

How do you determine your need to reveal confidential information?

- Reveal confidential information only if it is within your job responsibility to do so.

- Divulge confidential content based on each recipient's intended use of it, which should benefit your company in all cases.

- Reveal private information only if the owner consents.

Your Intuitive Inclination to Share

Under what circumstances should you reveal confidential or private information? Thousands of newcomers to my corporate information protection training sessions have answered this question honestly by confessing that they did not know. Those who admitted that their tendency is to share information rather than to ask themselves whether they should are not alone; they are like many people who are naturally inclined to be friendly, helpful, interesting, and even powerful by providing others information.

The primary goal of this chapter is to help you determine when it is appropriate to reveal confidential or private information. The secondary goal is to dissuade you from revealing such information unless it is for a purpose that benefits your company. The point is not to discourage sharing, interacting, or collaborating. Rather, it is to encourage navigating interactions to avoid causing harm to you or your company in the process. The answers to the following four questions determine when it is appropriate to disclose company confidential information:

- What is your role in disseminating company information?
- Who is asking?
- What is their need to know the information?
- What is the nature of the desired information?

I address each question individually.

What Is Your Role in Disseminating Company Information?

If you are a software developer, you are quite familiar with the software you are creating and the process of writing code with and for a specific application. What if someone from your company's public relations (PR) department decides to make an improvement—without asking and just because she thought she could—to change a few lines of your code? It seems wrong for an untrained, unauthorized person from PR to muck up your work in her attempt to make improvements, doesn't it?

Now imagine that you work in PR and a software engineer responds to questions from a journalist working for a software trade publication. The software engineer could easily muck up the company's PR strategy. Why would a software engineer, who is not trained or authorized to be a company spokesperson, respond to a journalist? It may be because he wants to demonstrate his expertise and be recognized. Or he may assume he is benefiting his company. Many believe that being an expert at what they do makes them an expert at talking about it with others. It does not. In fact, refusing to talk to a journalist about company confidential information may be a business-savvy indicator.

There is an efficiency that comes from knowing when you are on the line for divulging information and when you are not. You may be able to eliminate e-mails, phone calls, and meetings simply by referring requests for information to someone in your company whose job it is to respond to such requests. To gain this kind of efficiency—which benefits you and your organization—you first need to understand your role in company information dissemination.

Different elements of a workforce engage with the outside world in various ways. Typically, there are several clearly defined corporate functions whose job it is to share information. Public relations and corporate communications professionals are trained to speak to the press and the public. Legal counsel is authorized and qualified to speak for the company concerning legal matters. The sales force is pumped and primed to pitch the organization's products and services to prospects and customers. Finance and procurement personnel are trained and authorized to purchase goods and services.

Understanding your place in your company's information dissemination scheme will help you to know when it's your job to share information. It is usually straightforward and largely defined by job function. Once you understand your role, you will see there is a sphere of people to whom you are responsible for imparting information. Rather than responding directly to information requests that are outside your job, it is best to refer them to someone who is authorized to respond. Inquiries from reporters and industry analysts, for instance, should typically be passed on to the PR department.

Revealing information may be outside your job function because of the person requesting the information, the type of information requested, or the circumstances of the request. After reading this chapter, you may decide you only need to provide information about your work to your supervisor and a few employees and contractors on your team. Do you feel relieved? If not, you may be disappointed because you enjoy enhancing your company's public relations buzz, responding to journalists, participating in virtual worlds, blogging, or tweeting about your area of expertise. Your company may want you to be interactive if you understand what is confidential and the circumstances under which such information should and should not be shared. Your company may have guidelines for speaking to the press and participating in work-related blogs and other online interactive sites, and a representative from your company's PR department may be willing to train you to be an authorized company spokesperson.

If you are a software engineer, you wouldn't mind someone from PR writing a few lines of code after some training (and after you put some limits on what that person is authorized to do), would you? Someone in PR may appreciate you sharing your perspective with the outside world, but only after you have been instructed on how best to do so.

The Job of a Company Spokesperson

Communications professionals empowered to speak to the press and issue official statements must be on constant alert. When conducting a press conference, they must anticipate questions and the direction they may take, steering the conversation from treacherous terrain, guiding themselves and the company's executives or subject matter experts through a maze of inquiries, and dodging unwanted disclosure traps. Much of their training is preparing for such challenges. They are skilled in the martial arts of weaving stories and shaping images to influence hearts and minds. Those they interact with on a daily basis, including business reporters, industry analysts, and activists of various ideological persuasions, are also highly skilled, well informed, and quite possibly bent on leading communications professionals where they do not want to go. A PR professional's job is to give the best possible perception of her company, its people, and its products or services. The journalist's job is to get the inside scoop—uncover information and present it in a way that entices readers.

Executives must also cope with the challenge of releasing the news they intend to publicize at the optimum time. Their job is to keep their cool and adhere to their strategy wherever they are, including the greens of the golf course and the clay of the tennis court, whether they are wooing or being wooed. They have communications professionals to help them and legal professionals who weigh every word of their official statements.

Spokesperson vs. Representative

While official company spokespeople, such as the head of your company's PR department, chief legal counsel, and CEO, are authorized to speak on behalf of your company, and it is their job to respond to official questions from the media, every employee, including you, represents the company. You represent your company every time you make a statement, whether formal or informal, at an industry conference, trade show, or professional association meeting; on a blog, wiki, social networking site, listserv or video posted on YouTube; and with any other public or quasi-public communication you make outside your company. If you can be identified as a company employee, your statements and actions (or silence and inaction) may be attributed to you and your company, whether or not that is your intention. Consulting with your company's public relations or corporate relations department before you participate in any public or quasi-public forum will help you to achieve what you intend without diminishing yourself or your company.

Most companies require that you get approval before you make a public presentation, submit an article, or otherwise communicate with the public, such as at an industry-specific forum. Many companies also require that you get training before you participate in a collaboration, blog, or wiki with company outsiders. Such approval and training helps you avoid making inappropriate confidential information disclosures. It also helps ensure that whatever you say in public contributes to creating the best possible public image for your company. Both you and your company benefit when you avoid embarrassing blunders and instead take advantage of opportunities to bolster your company's persona. If you are in doubt about how best to present information in any public or quasi-public forum, you should ask an official company spokesperson.

Who Is Asking?

People will ask you for information because they believe you have information they seek. Possessing the information desired does not make it appropriate to share it. Rather, determining your need to divulge confidential information depends, in part, on who is asking for it.

Imagine this. It's early Monday morning, and you are feeling refreshed from the weekend. The telephone rings, and you answer it. The caller says he is a contractor who your company's vice president of quality assurance (QA) has just hired to assess and improve your company's chemical manufacturing processes. He wants to know what chemical compounds you have worked on lately, including the processes and timeframes. "Okay," you think to yourself. You are clearly authorized to speak with someone working for the VP of QA on issues related to chemical compound manufacturing. In fact, with all the problems you've had lately, you would like to work with this guy if he can help improve manufacturing processes.

How do you know the person on the other end of the telephone is a contractor that your company's VP of QA hired? Might he also be a contractor for your company's competitor? Perhaps your competitor hired him to get information that he will later use to dissuade your customers from buying your company's chemicals.

Many competitive intelligence professionals are experts at using social engineering ruses to get you to reveal sensitive information. Three of their most effective tools are

- Flattery: "The VP of QA said I could talk to any chemical engineer, but I've heard through the grapevine that you are number one in the company. Since I want to base my recommendations on the company's best practices, I want to talk to you."

- Sympathy: "The VP of QA has asked me to map out current specialty chemical manufacturing processes. I have a steep learning curve. I'd really appreciate your help."

- Urgency: "I've got twenty-four hours to deliver a report to the VP of QA. I'd like just twenty minutes of your time now so that I can include your comments in my report."

The requestor may use one or more of these ploys to get information from you. And when they fail, some information gatherers will use manipulation through intimidation, including threats and browbeating. "If you don't provide the information within an hour, I will personally let the VP of QA know you were uncooperative and prevented me from delivering the report he demanded."

Some attempts to collect sensitive information from you will come from unscrupulous people with their own ulterior motives, such as salespeople from a competing enterprise, headhunters scouting job placements, or stock prospectors looking for inside information. Some attempts may come from disgruntled employees (or ex-employees) who want to harm the organization and exact retribution for some perceived wrong.

In one case, Mansori Uekihara, a sales manager for Linear Technology-Japan, a computer chip manufacturer, showed up on a loading dock of a competing chip manufacturer, Maxim Integrated Products, impersonating an official from Toshiba, a significant Maxim customer. Mr.

Uekihara was well-dressed, confident, and articulate. He spoke with several Maxim product managers and asked them for datasheets and samples of a chip Maxim was developing. He was given an advance copy datasheet for an unreleased product and sent product engineering samples to his home address. Maxim became suspicious and ultimately learned about Mr. Uekihara's ruse only after it discovered that its competitor had given detailed information about Maxim's unreleased product to a customer.

Requests for information often come from people who look and sound courteous, professional, and official. Even before the 2010 United States census started, Census Bureau imposters were going door-to-door and asking for personal information. The United States Census Bureau had to warn residents to be cautious, indicating that Census Bureau workers would always have a badge, a handheld device, an official canvas bag, and a confidentiality notice when canvassing neighborhoods.

A request for information may be in person, over the telephone, or via e-mail. The request may be direct, or it may be an online post tempting your response. Requests for information may come from an e-mail address that looks authentic and legitimate because the name after the "@" symbol will direct you to a genuine-looking Web site. In the practice known as "phishing," these deceptive e-mails and Web sites are used to fish information out of people or companies. If you are in the travel clothing business, for example, and you receive an e-mail requesting information about upcoming product designs for climate change gear from Dina Jones at djones@weatherone.com, you might believe Dina is who she claims to be if there is a legitimate-looking

Web site at www.weatherone.com. Because it is easy and inexpensive to develop a Web site just to deceive people so they might disclose company information, you may be fooled.

Similar to requests from unknown individuals, a request for information that appears to come from an institution you trust may not be from them. Phishing often looks like an official e-mail, instant message, or tweet from a respected business, such as eBay, PayPal, or an online bank or credit card company where you may have an account. The e-mail directs you to a Web site that looks like, but is not, the Web site of the trustworthy entity. The Web site asks you for sensitive information, such as your user name, password, and credit card details. The information you enter is used to withdraw money from your accounts and make charges against your credit card. Phishing scams have targeted tens of millions of people. Each year, millions have responded and become identity theft victims. American victims are estimated to lose more than $3 billion annually. To see how wily the perpetrators can be, take a look at the following message I received in my corporate e-mail account:

Immediate Attention to All Account Users

Please be advised that there will be scheduled maintenance on all Internet and Intranet Web servers subscribers as well as the Email Servers on Saturday 16th and 23rd, 2010 beginning at 9:00 p.m. until approximately 12:00 midnight to enable us to increase the storage size of your account. All web and mail services will be interrupted during these periods. In order to avoid problems signing into your account after the maintenance; you are advised to send us your email account details. After upgrading, a password reset link will be sent to your email for new password. Furthermore, be informed that we will not hesitate to delete all email accounts that are not functioning, to create more space for new user. Please send us your mail account details as follows for confirmation.

*Email
*User Name
*Password

This is a scheduled maintenance period that will be occurring each month, due to the amount of junk email received daily.

Regards
ITS Helpdesk

The bad grammar and request for account details tipped me off to look in the headers. Because I do not use the Internet service provider that allegedly sent the e-mail, I immediately knew this was a phishing attempt and not a lawful request. Viewing full headers on e-mails helps to identify false addresses and automatic redirects from one Web site to another, a common practice involving fake Web sites.

Online scams using Twitter, called "twishing," include an incident where hundreds of thousands of Twitter users received either public replies or private tweets from followers that directed them to "this funny blog about you" followed by a link. When they clicked on the link, they were bounced away to a Twitter lookalike Web site at a different Web address where they were prompted to enter their login ID and password, which scammers could then use.

Regardless of the scenario, if you are not familiar with the individual or entity sending the online message, there are reasons to be suspicious. You can put the burden of identification on the requester by requiring he provide evidence that he is who he claims to be before you reply to the question or request for information. You might let him know that, because you do not know him and do not have authorization to reveal the information he is requesting unless you can verify who he is, you will need some proof of identity. You will also need to know that the information he is requesting will be used for the purpose he claims. In many cases, the best authenticator is a third person you both know who can vouch for the requestor and his need for the information.

"I'd be happy to talk to you about the processes I use to manufacture specialty chemicals," you might say. "All I will need is some communication directly from our VP of QA that you have been authorized to receive the information. Would you have him send me an e-mail to let me know you are authorized, or would you prefer that I discuss this with him directly?" You can be courteous when someone you don't know asks for confidential information even if you suspect he is not who he says he is.

It may take some courage and a bit of work, but before you make accessible any sensitive or private information you should be absolutely sure you know the real identity of the person requesting it and its intended use. If you know the person asking for confidential information and she makes her request or confirms it in person or via telephone, you can safely assume she is who she appears to be. A request sent via e-mail may not warrant the same response. In 2008, the Koobface virus was distributed in messages that appeared to be sent by friends, family, and trusted acquaintances through Facebook, MySpace, and Bebo social networks. While social networking sites are never an appropriate place to expose company confidential information, scams using those sites are another reason to question whether an e-mail that appears to be from someone in your social network has actually been sent by that person. Malicious software, known as malware (discussed in chapter 7) and used to send a virus through social networks, can also be used to issue requests for confidential company information from the people you trust.

Because phishing scams are so sophisticated, it is best to assume that any request for personal and account information made via e-mail, instant message, or tweet is a scam. Rather than trying to establish that an official-looking request for information is genuine and responding to an e-mail through the Web link provided, the safer course is to contact the company via telephone or log into the company's Web site by typing its Web address directly into your browser.

What Is the Requestor's Need to Know the Information?

Stakeholders need information about your company to contribute to its success. Contractors, vendors, temporary employees, customers, and others also want information because it contributes to their success, profit, sense of power, or capacity to retaliate against your organization. Your need to reveal company confidential information largely depends on the requestor's need to have it.

While it may be difficult to anticipate how the information will actually be used, you should be confident before you make confidential information available that the recipient genuinely needs it for a purpose that will serve your company.

If you think need is subjective, you are right. I have worked with companies whose senior executives believe that every employee *needs* access to all company information. Their philosophy is that it provides context and meaning for their employees' jobs and enables interdisci-plinary innovation in all areas of the company. Other clients mandate a separation of duties and allow information access and authorizations only for discrete work responsibilities. Compliance under corporate governance laws, such as Sarbanes-Oxley, also requires a separation of duties to prevent fraud such as what happened in the Enron corporate accounting scandal. Because "need" is a subjective concept defined differently by different companies, you may have to learn your compa-ny's definition to determine when you need to reveal confidential information and when the recipient has a need to receive it.

Regardless of company philosophy, there is often a tension between the scope of information that one should make available to provide context and the scope of information that makes the company unnec-essarily vulnerable. A consultant needs company information to be well-informed and understand your organization's problem set thor-oughly so she can help create desired solutions. The consultant will also likely use her experience from working with your company at her next engagement when working with your company's competitor. If you ponder the consultant's specific need to know information about her project, you may be able to reduce her access to your organization's secrets and thereby reduce their use in a future work assignment for another company.

One challenge is to understand that the mix of another person's curiosity and interest, combined with your inclination to be friendly, helpful, or interesting, can be dangerous. Information is like fertile topsoil that nurtures business innovation and growth. If your company is successful, there will be a lot of curiosity, both from within and outside your company, to learn what is in that topsoil. Yet curiosity and interest do not establish that the person or organization that wants information actually needs it.

Technology Makes Overextending (Too) Easy

Communication technologies that make information sharing easy amplify the danger of sharing too much. Consider, for example, the simple act of adding someone when you reply to an e-mail message thread because the new person's expertise or interests are now germane to some discussion in the e-mail. All the correspondence included in that e-mail thread will be available to the new addressee. There may be information in that thread that should not be exposed blithely. Deleting the sections of an e-mail conversation that are not required by all of the e-mail recipients may be a slightly inconvenient but fitting step to keep confidential information from those who do not need it.

Similarly, if you choose reply all, you will be sending your reply and any included e-mail stream to all recipients of the original e-mail. Do you intend for each addressee to read not only your reply, but also the entire e-mail conversation? It may be better to hit reply instead of reply all to limit the recipients of your message.

Both e-mail and voice messaging technologies make it easy to mistakenly share information with unintended recipients who have no need for the information. Have you ever received a voice message that was clearly intended for someone else? Many people have.

It is easy to send information to the wrong person. In 2002, the Pew Internet and American Life project reported that 10 percent of so-called work e-mailers had accidently sent an embarrassing e-mail to the wrong person at work. By the time the Marlin Company released its annual Attitudes in the American Workplace study in 2007, that percentage had doubled.

If you are creating a message and the e-mail application includes an automatic recall function that anticipates the address you are typing, it is easy to send an e-mail to the wrong Susan. For every e-mail sent, there are several opportunities to make this mistake in the To, CC (carbon copy), and BCC (blind carbon copy) fields.

Because of a typo in the address line, former Walt Disney CEO Michael Eisner inadvertently sent Disney's earnings report to an ABC News employee before its public release date. He said

> I have come to believe that if anything will bring about the downfall of a company, or maybe even a country, it is blind copies of e-mails that should never have been sent in the first place. Of course, the SEC wouldn't have laughed if the earnings had leaked out to someone at ABC News who traded in our stock. (Associated Press, 5/12/00)

Justifications and Standards for Sharing Confidential and Private Information

The ultimate question is whether, in your company's business philosophy, there is a valid justification for sharing the information with each person with whom you share it. If there is an expected benefit that supports your company, then there is a good reason to share the information. If such a business case does not exist and the intended recipient does not require the confidential information in order to benefit your company, you should not reveal it.

There is an even stricter standard for private information. Many privacy laws require that your company obtain written permission from the individual information owner before you can legally distribute personally identifiable information, such as employee or customer names and preferences, outside your company.

Revealing confidential or private information is never rationalized simply by virtue of a signed NDA and a prospective recipient's interest in knowing the information. The NDA establishes a relationship of trust, not a reason to reveal.

What Is the Nature of the Desired Information?

The justification threshold is higher for more sensitive information. The more sensitive the information, the more cautious you should be about making it available. A company's source code development, its manufacturing process, or its acquisition plans, for example, should be made known only with those few people who are involved in those tasks. On the other hand, confidential cost information might be shared with a broader group of people working to reduce the company's overall expenses.

If a contractor helping you to evaluate pricing models requests the formula used to calculate large order discounts, you should be confident prior to giving any confidential information that it will be useful to carry out his work on your project. If the contractor insists that he needs access to the database with all customer accounts, including product prices and payment terms for each, you should apply a higher level of scrutiny. If the contractor could evaluate pricing models without full access to your company's customer database, then it's probably best not to provide full access to it. You might ask the contractor to justify his need for each type of information available in the database. If he cannot provide it, then you might make arrangements through your company's IT organization to allow him access to only the specific data fields he actually needs and will use for his project with you.

The information classifications discussed in chapter 4 should help you know which information is more sensitive and, therefore, when to apply the higher level of scrutiny. The formula used to calculate discounts given to your company's largest clients might be classified as "Company Confidential," while the customer database, which includes all customer accounts, product prices, and payment terms for each, is more sensitive and might be classified as "Company Confidential: Special Handling." The higher-level classification is a signal that a higher level of scrutiny—a stronger rationalization based on a specific business necessity—is required before divulging the information.

Generally, the more detailed or comprehensive the information, the more sensitive it is. If you can achieve your objectives by giving a less detailed, less complete, or less sensitive version of confidential information, it is advisable to do so.

Familiarity with confidential information protection requirements helps save time and effort. Because less sensitive information requires less vigilance, the less sensitive the information you share, the less caution you need to apply. Sharing confidential information only when you are responsible for doing so and then sharing only the least sensitive information needed can make you more efficient and effective. It also frees up your time and attention to share, interact, and collaborate using known nonconfidential information.

Developing a Sixth Sense and Activating Your Internal Filter

Unfortunately, no external alarm triggers when our in-person or online conversations traverse the line between nonconfidential and confidential content. It is easy to let some sensitive information slip in casual conversation (at the office, a party, the beach, or an airport lounge) whatever strata of a company's workforce you toil in, whether you are in human resources, operations, sales, engineering, media or analyst relations, the legal office, or even (and especially) if you have a seat on the board of directors.

Similarly, no automatic shutoff valve prevents requests for information from those who have no valid need for it. As you make sales calls or receive such calls, develop the specifications for a new product, or analyze others' products, the people with whom you interact are going to ask questions. And, in the course of your daily workflow, as you sit at a laboratory workstation until your back aches, travel from client to client until the jet lag overtakes you, or stand in trade show booths until your soles burn, your job undoubtedly requires that you respond.

In many cases, the questions and requests for information come from co-workers and people outside your firm, including customers, potential clients, business partners, suppliers, building maintenance personnel, and consultants. The medium of your conversation could be verbal or digital, in-person, or virtual. The person with whom you are in conversation could be someone you know well, but nevertheless, has no need to know confidential company information. Some of what she asks for may be used to serve your company while some may be used in ways that are ill-intended and dangerous to your company's well-being. The person with whom you are chatting could be deliberately trying to collect information that will be used to destroy your relationships with customers. Or the person could have no ill intention toward you or your company, but nevertheless, will expose the information you share with her, perhaps even unintentionally, in some way that harms you and your organization. Or the person could use the information solely and exclusively to perform a task that helps your company. It takes both knowing the facts and having a strong intuition to anticipate which of these is true in the circumstance you face.

Imagine this. It's Friday evening. As you are clearing off your desk and shutting down your computer after a long week, you have one eye on the clock. You do not want to miss the 6:30 PM train. A desperately-needed weekend at the shore awaits you. The phone rings. You can tell by the sound of the ring that it is an internal call. Seemingly friendly and flustered, the person on the other end says, "I'm Ted Good. I've put together a negotiation strategy for a secret deal the executives are working on right now. I know you are one of the most respected administrative assistants in the company. I really need your help to get me contact information—cell phone, e-mail, and hotel information—for the senior executives so they can review my report. I've got to get it to them tonight, or they won't be able to implement my recommendations."

What do you do? Those you would ask for guidance after putting the caller on hold have all left for the weekend. The executives you might approach with a tap on their door are already in flight, winging off to an important transatlantic conference, perhaps related to the caller's query. Though you are rushed and pressed to do the right thing fast, you hopefully stop a moment to run through a simple four-question mental checklist:

- Are you authorized to share the requested information with the intended recipient?
- Is the intended recipient who he claims to be?
- Does the intended recipient need the information to benefit your company?
- How can you reveal the least amount of sensitive information to achieve the intended purpose?

As an administrative assistant to executives, you may be authorized to provide the executives' contact information to consultants working for them. If the person calling is a stranger to you, you should have a healthy dose of suspicion about whether he is really working at the request of company executives. Still, there is no reason to be discourteous. Instead, without imparting any confidential information, you can suggest to Mr. Good that he provide you with his contact information. You can then leave a message for your boss letting her know about the call and the request for information. If your boss wants the report, she or you can call Mr. Good and have him send it directly to her. Your boss can then forward the report to the other executives.

The mental checklist is easy and painless. It allows you to catch your breath and your train. It makes you look good to your boss, and it helps you protect your company's valuable intellectual assets.

For many people, this response is counterintuitive. Our human nature is to share information when we are asked. Our inclination is to take on the pressure when a request for information seems urgent. Perhaps you had a professional colleague or counterpart from a competing company ask you about something at a trade show or business conference, or maybe you received a call asking you to participate in a survey or benchmark study. The temptation to talk about what is on the drawing board or under wraps can feel overpowering.

Many are unclear about how best to respond when dealing with the tension between temptation and resistance. The most effective guide in these situations is an internal filter that you can develop to sense when you should or should not reveal confidential information. The first step is to just pause, take a breath, and review the four-question mental checklist enumerated previously. The business world is moving at a relentless pace. Still, there is always one breath's worth of time to do a self-check. Is the dialogue going in a direction that could become problematic? Are you controlling your disclosures?

Whether you are making an in-person sales pitch, speaking on the phone, writing a text message, participating in an online chat room, engaging in cocktail conversation, being looped into an e-mail thread, responding in a conference Q&A session, conducting a job interview, or, conversely, being interviewed for a job, there is always enough time to pause and run through an internal filter checklist.

It is often helpful to externalize your questions and concerns. "I'm not sure I'm authorized to give you that information," you might say. "I will need to know a little more about you, how you plan to use the information, and if there is some less sensitive information that might be equally suitable." The more sensitive the information, the more acute the recipient's need for the information must be, and the more compelling the business case should be to justify the disclosure.

Countless encounters should trigger your sixth sense and your internal information discretion filter. The point is not to live your life on high alert or to become consumed by paranoia. The point is to adapt and integrate a common sense internal filtering process that fits your temperament and business environment. As we will explore in chapter 8, the sixth sense needed to trigger your internal filter is already operating in many aspects of your life. If you train yourself to draw on that same sixth sense in the information protection dimension of your professional life, it will help you to think on your feet and respond quickly. You gain advantage from determining your need to reveal before you share confidential information. With some practice, the internal filter becomes second nature. People who are good at it find they are more effective in all their interactions, not just those involving company information protection.

Chapter 5 Spot Quiz
Determine Your Need to Reveal Before You Share Confidential Information

(The answer key can be found in appendix D)

Which of the following facts do you need to establish in order to evaluate your need to reveal confidential information?

A. You have to know what the nature of the information is; that is, how it has been classified within your company and what controls are supposed to be utilized for its protection.

B. You have to know if you are authorized to provide the information to those who have a need to know it.

C. You need to identify the person independent of his own claim.

D. All of the above

Is the following statement true or false?

Only your company spokesperson has to worry about what he says in public. The press and business analysts will only quote official sources.

Limit
Confidential Information
Exposure

CHAPTER 6

Chapter 6 Takeaways

How do you limit confidential information exposure?

- Create safe zones, where you cannot be overheard by eavesdroppers or seen by unintended onlookers, before sharing confidential information.

- Minimize the confidential information available in unsafe zones.

- Be conscious and conscientious, remembering that everything you say or do may be a clue to your company's secrets.

Information Exposure and the Germ Theory

Imagine for a moment that you have a cold. Out of respect and concern for those around you, you don't want to pass it on. Let's assume you ascribe to the germ theory, believing that germs spread illness, particularly the common cold. To reduce exposing others to your cold, you might avoid going to public places and touching things that others may touch. When in a public place, you might cover your mouth with a tissue and turn your head when you need to sneeze. If you do need to touch something that others may touch, such as a doorknob to a public restroom or the handlebar on the grocery store shopping cart, you might apply an antibacterial sanitizer gel or wash what you touch or your hands before and after use.

Limiting confidential information exposure is similar because information is like a germ. Our very presence can spread it, as can the myriad ways we communicate and send signals to the outside world. In addition to revealing confidential information intentionally (chapter 5), we expose information germs unknowingly. An expression on your face may register as disapproval or disagreement to something about which you have stated you have "no comment." A luggage tag or logo on your T-shirt may reveal context to the stories you thought you told confidentially because you did not mention anyone's name. And even the number of pizzas you order for delivery to a conference room in your company's manufacturing building may reveal that a product launch is imminent. In one case, local journalists accurately predicted my client's product release date based on the large number of pizzas ordered after nine o'clock at night that were delivered to the company's manufacturing facility. The journalists befriended the owner of my client's favorite pizza restaurant and paid him $20 to alert them about large pizza delivery orders after business hours.

Protecting information is like protecting others from catching your cold. The best way to keep your germs from spreading is to stay home and say and do nothing. While this strategy may protect others from catching your germs and keep you from exposing your company's confidential information, it is in neither your own nor your company's interests to follow it, particularly if you have a drive to be active in the world and engaged with others.

So how do you balance your interest in limiting exposure with your interest in being a lively participant in life's activities? One golden rule applies: Be aware that exposure creates a risk that you should keep in check. And, unlike the germs that cause your cold, many people are interested in catching your information (chapter 2). They are seeking it aggressively. Everything you do or don't do, say or don't say, and reveal or don't reveal may illuminate confidential information for someone receptive to its light.

Think of information germs as being pieces of a puzzle, like the ones shown in figure 1. Someone somewhere—and likely many people in many places—are collecting puzzle pieces from you and others in order to uncover a picture of you, your company, or some aspect of what you do or how you do it. As with the typical common cold, you don't need to stay home and do nothing out of fear that you might spread your germs. Instead, you can be conscientious when you are out in the world so you limit disseminating your germs or your company's confidential information.

Ground Zero for Confidential Information Exposure

Ground zero, the epicenter of your confidential information exposure, is your work environment, which may be physical or virtual. In this chapter, we focus on the physical work environment while in chapter 7, I address digital security basics for the electronic work environment.

Your physical work environment is fluid. It may be your office, your home, a customer's facility, an airplane, and a hotel room all in the same day. Physical security for these environments requires more than a lock on a door and a fence around a building. Information can be seen through a window, heard as keystrokes on a mobile phone, and intuited from a "Welcome" sign in a hotel lobby. You can keep germs of confidential information secure in these environments by

- Creating safe zones, where you cannot be overheard by eavesdroppers or seen by unintended onlookers, before sharing any confidential information

- Minimizing the confidential information available in unsafe zones

Confidential Information Exposure

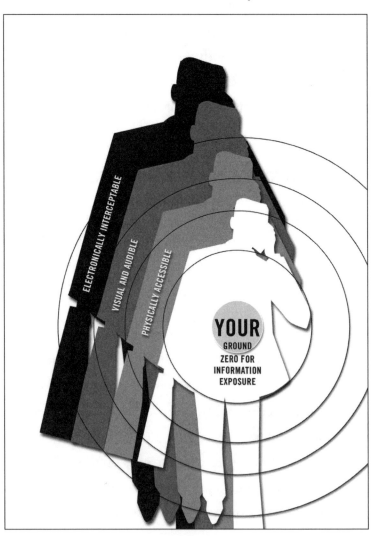

Figure 5

I will soon demonstrate how you can conduct an appraisal of the information vulnerabilities in your work environments to accomplish these two goals. A primary objective is to maintain control over information exposure from your ground zero, keeping in mind the potential for information compromise and loss (chapter 2). Using the concentric circles of possible access, diagramed in figure 5, you can appraise how you are exposing confidential information germs from your physical, mobile, and fluid work environments. By consciously appraising your information exposure, you retain the choice to take calculated risks rather than subject yourself and your company to the perils that occur when you inadvertently divulge information in an unsafe zone.

Public areas are generally unsafe, particularly if other people are close by. It may be impossible to create a safe zone in a site where it is uncertain who is or may soon be present, such as in a restaurant, lobby, or commuter train. Unintended eavesdroppers, as well as corporate spies and journalists, may be tempted to listen and watch.

A woman sitting outside a coffee shop enjoying her Sunday morning latte overheard an executive in the company where her husband worked talking nearby on his cell phone. The executive was relaying his news that he may soon be leaving the company. Rumors of his separation soon spread, both in the company and to customers and business partners. Instead, the executive stayed at the company, but had to counter the rumors and was less effective for months because of them.

The executive's choice to have his conversation outside the café may have been an attempt to minimize his risk of being overheard inside the crowded restaurant. Because the executive could not create a safe zone, the best he could do was to decrease the number of potential eavesdroppers. But a less crowded site may still be an unsafe zone where the risks are greater than the potential gain of having a conversation at that place and time. When you choose to share confidential information under these circumstances, it is like going to the office, despite your contagious low-grade fever, sniffling, coughing, and sneezing, to do work with your team that could be done from home. Especially when exposure poses risks that exceed the potential reward, you should do whatever you can to reduce or eliminate it.

It will be helpful if you understand what kinds of potential information exposures you should be concerned about and why. The following table provides a useful sampling of the ways you may be exposing confidential information and includes some of the concerns you should take into account to minimize potential information leaks. The last column summarizes some of the precautions you might take to address the exposures and concerns.

Precautions to Address Information Exposures & Concerns from Your Ground Zero

Potential Exposure from WHAT YOU DO	Concerns	Precautions
Words you speak ("loose lips"), particularly in places other than a private office, such as airplanes, airports, lobbies, restaurants, gyms, or at home	– May be overheard by eavesdroppers	– Be cautious about what you say, particularly in semi-public or public places
Facial expression(s)	– May register unintended information, for example, disapproval, alarm, or acceptance	– Be aware of your nonverbal reactions
E-mail, text message, Facebook, Twitter, or other electronic transmissions	– May be sent to the wrong addressee – May be sent to individuals on the distribution list who do not have a need for the information in the message – May include more information than the recipients on an e-mail or text stream need – May be intercepted	– Check recipient addresses and numbers – Confirm that all recipients are intended – Review e-mail and text stream and delete information that recipients do not need – Encrypt confidential e-mail transmission if it is sent over a nonsecure network, such as the Internet

Precautions to Address Information Exposures & Concerns from Your Ground Zero *(continued)*		
Potential Exposure from WHAT YOU DO	**Concerns**	**Precautions**
Voicemail	– Confidential messages may be forwarded to unintended recipients – Messages may be listened to by those who guess the voice-mail password	– Select the private option when available for confidential outgoing voice messages – Limit the confidential information left in a voicemail message and state in the message that it is confidential – Use strong voicemail passwords
Mail	– May be read or taken by those who should not have access to the information	– Use an opaque envelope or protective cover to conceal confidential information – Indicate "to be opened by addressee only" on an outer envelope and "confidential" on an inner envelope
Food delivery orders	– May indicate unusual circumstances, such as an imminent product release, if the order is, for example, late at night or larger quantities than usual	– Ask the food service provider to keep the fact of your order confidential

Precautions to Address Information Exposures & Concerns from Your Ground Zero *(continued)*		
Potential Exposure from WHAT YOU USE	**Concerns**	**Precautions**
Mobile phone, personal digital assistant (PDA), laptop, USB drive, or other mobile device	– Conversations and keystrokes may be overheard by eavesdroppers – May be lost or stolen – May allow information access by whomever finds or steals the device	– Make phone calls in as private an area as possible – Use speed dial numbers – Keep mobile devices in a secure place where they won't fall out (in a pocket) or be picked up by a passerby (in a lockable drawer or cabinet) – Cable lock your laptop to something that is hard to remove – Lock the door to any room where electronic devices are left unattended
Fax machine, printer, and photocopier	– Documents may be read or picked up by someone other than the intended recipient	– Pick up faxed or printed documents as soon as they are available – Notify recipients when you send a fax so they can pick it up immediately – Be careful to enter in the correct fax number
Whiteboards and flip charts	– May allow others who can see the whiteboard or flip chart, including through a window or open door, to read what is written on it	– Erase or shred when the information is no longer needed – Block whiteboards and flip charts from being visible through windows and open doors

Precautions to Address Information Exposures & Concerns from Your Ground Zero *(continued)*		
Potential Exposure from WHAT YOU USE	**Concerns**	**Precautions**
Repositories of confidential documents and other confidential materials, including file cabinets, your desk, your car trunk, and your briefcase	— Information or the repository (your briefcase or car) may be taken by someone who should not have access to the information	— Keep information repositories locked and away from easy reach — Break up large amounts of confidential materials when practical so the loss of some information does not result in the loss of all of it
Speakerphone	— Voicemail messages and conversations may be overheard by eavesdroppers	— Use speakerphones only in private
A luggage tag, name tag, or logo on your clothing	— May reveal context or identify players in the stories you thought you told in confidence because you did not mention anyone's name	— If you have luggage tags or logos on your clothing that reveal your company affiliation, be particularly careful about what you say
Photocopy shop	— Sensitive documents may be read by photocopy shop staff — Copies of sensitive documents may be made available to other patrons	— Request that only one person at the photocopy shop handle your project, and inform her that the project is confidential and any imperfect copies should be returned to you or shredded — Require an NDA when suitable

Precautions to Address Information Exposures & Concerns from Your Ground Zero *(continued)*		
Potential Exposure from YOUR ENVIRONMENT	**Concerns**	**Precautions**
Transparent office windows or open doors	– Information on white-boards, computer screens, and bulletin boards may be visible from the outside – Meeting participants may be identified and photographed	– Turn or cover confidential information displays so they are not visible from office windows or open doors – Use window coverings to prevent outsiders from identifying or photographing meeting participants
Cubicles or open or thin-walled offices	– Conversations and keystrokes may be overheard	– Close office doors, whisper, and check surroundings before speaking in confidence
Airplane, bus, train, taxi, or other public transportation	– Conversations may be overheard by the driver or other travelers – May unintentionally leave documents and devices containing confidential informa-tion (PDAs, mobile phones, USB drives, laptops, iPads, or DVDs) with no way to retrieve them	– If you must discuss confidential information on public transportation, do it in code or a whisper – Hand-carry documents and devices while trav-eling, and label them with minimal contact information for return if they are lost – Password protect or encrypt devices – Use software that allows remote data deletion and lockout if the device is lost or stolen

Precautions to Address Information Exposures & Concerns from Your Ground Zero *(continued)*		
Potential Exposure from YOUR ENVIRONMENT	**Concerns**	**Precautions**
Unsecured work areas, such as at home, in a hotel, on a wireless hot spot, or in a customer's facility	– Confidential information may be seen or taken by those who should not have access to it	– Access or expose confidential information in unsecured work areas as infrequently and minimally as is practical
Unneeded hard copies (document drafts)	– May be read or taken by those who should not have access to the information	– Avoid making unneeded copies – Destroy, such as by shredding, unneeded copies – Check with your records department to determine if copies are needed, and, if so, store them in a secure, restricted access file

Table 4

Potential Information Exposures Are Ubiquitous

In the twenty-first century, the cautionary reminder of "loose lips sink ships" is not just about what you say to whom, but also about where, when, and how you say it. As you work and play, you potentially expose company secrets. A secret once exposed may be lost forever.

The person to whom you confide sensitive information may indeed be trustworthy and have a need to know the information you share, but if you confide it in a conversation at a convention center lounge, over dinner at a busy restaurant, or in the backseat of a taxicab, you may inadvertently make secrets known to those who might sell them to your competitors or otherwise exploit them and cause harm to your enterprise.

It is not just loose lips, but also hurried fingers, distracted minds, jet-lagged bodies, and gullible egos that can literally and metaphorically expose secrets and sink ships. Your hurried fingers can accidently send a sensitive e-mail message to a potential client or an entire list of people in your industry who should not have access to the message's contents. Your distracted mind can leave hard copies of sensitive documents in a printer at a twenty-four-hour copy shop the night before an important regulatory hearing. Your jet-lagged body can slump over in exhaustion between flights somewhere while your PDA falls to the floor and buzzes with incoming e-mail. A competitor on her way to the same trade show where you are headed can pick it up and peruse its contents.

Creating safe zones for confidential information and minimizing confidential information exposure in unsafe zones can be challenging in a world where sensitive information is vulnerable no matter where you are, what you do, or how you do it—whether you are using the most rudimentary or technologically-advanced devices.

A Seemingly Insignificant Tidbit Can Be the Final Piece of a Strategic Puzzle

Technology makes it possible for vital and explicating information to be no more than a click or two away. While the publicly available information in blogs, executive speeches, regulatory filings, and webcasts may not, in and of itself, be confidential, each individual fact and opinion is elucidating. Once the puzzle's basic framework is in position, those interested in getting the whole picture can invest their resources in a focused attempt to obtain the missing pieces. If you are momentarily careless, what you depict may be exactly what is needed to complete a vivid picture of your company. It takes only one over-heard conversation on an airplane, one diagram left on a whiteboard, or one confidant who cannot keep a secret to provide the missing puzzle piece, as discussed previously. A seemingly unimportant state-ment, file, or visible clue may be the key that unlocks your company's secrets. While sharing information germs is often worth the risk, it is also worth the time and effort to consciously determine how to mini-mize or avoid potential peril.

Anyone interested will aggregate all the publicly available information about you and your company with the seemingly insignificant informa-tion that you reveal as well as the information leaked by others in your organization and extended enterprise. Using table 2 "Calculation of Confidential Information Exposures Per Day Per 1,000 Employees," we can extrapolate that twenty inadvertent confidential information exposures per day multiplied by two hundred and fifty working days equals five thousand opportunities per year for anyone interested in a one thousand-employee company's confidential information to hear it, see it, pick it up, copy it, or intercept it.

Such projections are arguably conservative. With electronic commu-nications, especially e-mail, wireless transfers, and mobile device transmissions of voice and data, and the interactive pull of social networking sites, blogs, wikis, and virtual worlds, the potentially accessible information transfers are exponentially higher. Each of these can be the missing piece needed to complete a scout's puzzle that uncovers your company's secrets. Each can be the loose lip that sinks your company's ship.

Your Personal Information Exposure Assessment

Evaluating confidential information exposure using the concentric circles of access concept (figure 5) will help create safe zones. You can do the evaluation in three simple steps.

First, assess your work location and the physical security of confidential information. Look around your desk or other work area(s) and ask

- Is it a safe space where confidential information can be seen only by those with whom you intend to share it and not onlookers, such as unplanned visitors and passersby?
- How is confidential information exposed?
  - Is it on a whiteboard or flip chart, near a window or in an open conference room?
  - Is it left out on your desk in the form of reports, prototypes, or notes?
  - Are electronic devices, particularly mobile devices, such as USB drives and DVDs, easily picked up by a passerby?

If the answer to the last two questions is yes, you can use a secure receptacle, such as a lockable drawer or cabinet to store documents, small devices, and removable electronic memory. To be prudent, only you and a backup, such as your manager or assistant, should have the key or lock combination.

You can minimize the sensitive information available in potentially unsafe zones by erasing whiteboards and removing confidential information from conference rooms before leaving them. You might cable lock your laptop to your desk or other fixed object and lock office and storage room doors to create a safe site for your unattended work product.

Second, as you go through this process, look for drafts and other unneeded copies of documents in hard copy and electronic form. If you discover them, check with your company's records retention manager or legal counsel to determine if there is a legal requirement to keep the documents and files. If there is no such requirement, you can destroy what you do not need. If there is a requirement to keep documents you don't currently use, store them in a secure, restricted access area. Like cleaning your closet of clothes you don't wear, cleaning your physical and electronic workspaces of confidential information you aren't using can shed a welcome light on what you have and value. By getting rid of what you don't need *and* discarding it securely, you also eliminate the risks of making it available to someone who should not have access to it. Confidential material thrown in a waste receptacle may be taken and used in harmful ways unless the contents are destroyed and are not accessible to others in the interim. Destroying confidential material in a secure manner may require shredding documents, breaking DVDs, or demagnetizing hard drives.

Third, consider how you share confidential information. Can you impart it in a safe zone to only the person or people with whom you intend to share it? How might you be overheard in your cubicle, on your cell phone, at the train station, or in a restaurant? Check to determine if anyone who peeks over your shoulder, glances into your office, peers through a conference room window, or glimpses your open briefcase can see confidential information. Take into account that the confidential information you transmit electronically over a nonsecure network can be copied, intercepted, or forwarded. If unencrypted, an unintended recipient can read it (discussed in chapter 7). Creating a safe zone requires eliminating unintended and unnecessary access to the confidential information you intend to share.

Governments and corporations hire professionals to probe both physical and cyber security to determine their respective organization's vulnerabilities. Security experts look for potential risks that need to be eliminated or at least narrowed to tolerable levels. While you may not be responsible for assessing and reducing risk and creating safe zones for confidential information at the organizational level, evaluating and limiting your own confidential information exposure is your job, no matter what your title or job description. Every employee is expected to meet this responsibility continuously. Each time your work area changes, as it follows you to the company break room, your car, or your daughter's soccer field sidelines, you are responsible for assessing and limiting the information exposure you create.

24-7 Vigilance in a 24-7 World

Constantly assessing and limiting information exposure is easy with the right mindset. From the corporate spy's perspective, your workspace has multiple information access points, coming in and going out, both physically and digitally, including through your computer, cell phone, PDA, USB drives, incoming mail, interoffice mail, the in- and outbox on your desk, your desk itself, the fax machine, file cabinets in your office, and your briefcase or backpack.

If you follow confidential information as it flows in from one contact point, is handled or accessed in some way by you, and then flows out to another contact point, you can gauge whether it is flowing in from and out to safe zones that minimize exposure. Each contact point along the way is an opportunity to limit or eliminate potential confidential information vulnerability.

A hypothetical example may be helpful to illustrate the information exposure assessment process. Imagine your PDA chiming with text messages and buzzing with new e-mail messages while the telephone on your desk is ringing off the hook. You just hit send on your fax machine for a lengthy outgoing document. You glance down and observe that your inbox on your desk is almost overflowing. Meanwhile, you are using your laptop for Internet browsing and e-mail. Both applications are open. You are toggling back and forth between surfing the Internet, where you are researching a current project, and finishing off a lengthy e-mail response to a potential contractor's initial proposal on another project. Co-workers are dropping into your office to chitchat, hoping to pick up some gossip on a third project.

Your briefcase is open on the floor next to your swivel chair. You have stuffed it with several files that you hope to read over the weekend. The file cabinet drawer that those files came from is still open. Jotted on the whiteboard in the conference room across from your office are some product specifications summarized during a video conference you participated in earlier that day and some branding ideas from an impromptu brainstorming session late last night.

In this hypothetical example, you start your assessment of how information flowing in and out may be leaked or diverted by asking the simple question, "Are all of my confidential information exposures necessary?" If not, you should eliminate or at least reduce them.

Ready? Here goes. You wipe the whiteboard clean, perhaps first taking note of the contents in a word processing document, which you protect with a password. You close the file cabinet drawer and then lock the cabinet. You empty the fax machine inbox by bringing its contents to a file on your desk. As you are doing so, you realize you need to be more attentive when sending faxes. It would be easy to type in the wrong fax number, and it would be easier still to punch in the wrong preprogrammed number. You lock your briefcase and make a mental note to treat the files you are taking home with extra care throughout the weekend. You promise yourself not to leave them in your car trunk if you go out to dinner. You remove the confidential budget draft from your trash can and put it in the locked "to be shredded" bin in the hallway.

The following Monday, when working from a hotel, you leave for the evening without your laptop, which you secure with a cable lock affixed to an unmovable piece of furniture in your hotel room. You either turn it off or leave it on with a password-login screensaver running on it. Otherwise, someone cleaning your room, someone posing as you to disarm the person cleaning your room, or someone posing as a person cleaning your room could read the information you left available in your hurry to be on time for your restaurant reservation. Before you leave the restaurant that inspired your thinking, you take the paper napkins on which you jotted notes.

Does this sound difficult? It is not. Assessing and reducing your information exposure is easy once you look at your work environment with eyes that see the information germs you disseminate.

The Benefits of Reducing Confidential Information Exposure

Reducing confidential information exposure is likely to leave your desk, meeting rooms, and whiteboards cleaner and less cluttered. You may be more courteous (quieter and more discreet) when talking on a cell phone. There are less obvious benefits, too. Limiting exposure results in not suffering the harm that you have avoided. You will be more efficient and effective because there will be fewer rumors, less embarrassment, and smaller losses.

When you limit exposure by resuming a confidential discussion that started over lunch at your company cafeteria in a private conference room, you avoid the risk that the contractor at the nearby cafeteria table may use the information on a competing project with another company. Similarly, if you designate your outgoing voicemail messages as "private," you avoid the embarrassment of having confidential information forwarded to listeners that you did not intend. As we will explore in chapter 8, physical security and reducing information exposure are essential elements in your precautionary force field.

Follow the Currents of Information Coming and Going

Confidential information may be exposed not only as it flows out from your ground zero, but also, like germs, as information and other things flow in. Malicious code, such as a computer virus or spyware, can corrupt valuable information. We discuss these vulnerabilities in chapter 7. Taking in confidential information owned by another person or company can taint you, your company, and its products. If you have access to another company's confidential information without the owner's permission, your company can be stopped from selling any product or service that incorporates that information. We discuss this vulnerability in chapter 9. The point here is that, as you assess confidential information exposures from your ground zero to the outside world, you should also assess confidential information contamination from outside influences that may penetrate your actual or virtual workplace. Confidential information is like a germ that you want to spread or allow in only when it enhances your company's health.

Your Mindset Is a Powerful Ally

Limiting information exposure requires vigilance, but it is easy with the right outlook. All it takes is focusing your awareness on the ways that you make confidential information potentially accessible to others and the ways that others' information germs may infect you. If you are conscientious, you will see the clues, hints, evidence, and potential puzzle pieces your comments, tweets, posture, e-mails, phone messages, and luggage tags reveal.

Describing to a stranger you meet at an industry networking meeting, in general terms, the nature of a project you are working on may seem insignificant, but if your name tag lets the stranger know who you work for and she can learn other details about the project on a company blog, that same conversation may be detrimental to your company's well-being.

In today's interactive, blogged, and wiki-ed world, many people are interested in the clues, hints, and evidence you make available. Your professional impression depends, in part, on your ability to manage the information attributable to you. If you unintentionally expose information by discussing a customer's service needs on a cell phone while waiting at the train station, you may return to the office to find that a competitor has posted a comment about your call in an industry blog. You need to learn twenty-first century rules for a twenty-first century game, and you need 24-7-365 vigilance in a 24-7-365 world.

How do you maintain 24-7-365 vigilance while allowing yourself a life of your own and a decent night's sleep? It is easy. The answer lies in your sixth-sense approach to protecting information. You already create a behavior code, all mostly second nature, that enables you to function in the world as who and what you choose to be. You avoid walking in high-crime neighborhoods alone at night, you try to get some exercise and eat healthy food, and you dress and groom yourself to look your best for work and your social life. These protocols for your safety, health, and the impression you make with your physical presence are based on optimizing potential benefits and minimizing potential pitfalls. Similarly, you can adopt practices for reducing confidential information loss risks, which will improve your own and your company's well-being and prosperity, as well as enhance your professional reputation. Such practices involve creating safe zones and being discrete.

Walk on Rice Paper without Leaving a Footprint

The metaphor of walking on rice paper without leaving a footprint comes from the martial arts world to describe mastering stealth and subtlety. A master can walk on rice paper without leaving a footprint by tuning in to the right balance of essentials and environment. You can achieve similar skills for today's business environment without years of rigorous training in a Shaolin temple.

The risk reduction practices described in this chapter can, like your personal behavior code, become second nature. Just ask yourself, "How do I expose information to being taken, seen, heard, or intercepted?" The answer will help you assess and then limit your confidential information vulnerabilities.

You cannot know the repercussions of every act or omission, nor can you personally control every detail of a collaborative project. Your information world is an ecosystem with many interconnecting elements, including interested people and available information, that can impact you and your company in surprising and sometimes dangerous ways. By engaging a sixth sense, you follow the information flow in and out of your physical and cyber workspace, wherever that may be in an office or on the road, probing for the blind spots, the weak points, and the gaps that expose information. Then, when you perceive vulnerabilities, you can reduce or even eliminate them.

Looking at your environment with new eyes, you can learn to walk on rice paper without leaving a confidential information footprint. Limiting confidential information exposures enhances the confidentiality and value of that information. Every precaution you take to reduce a potential unintended confidential information disclosure mitigates the information loss risk and optimizes opportunities for gain.

Chapter 6 Spot Quiz
Limit Confidential Information Exposure

(The answer key can be found in appendix D)

Which of the following may expose information to risk?

A. A luggage tag

B. A request for proposal

C. Your travel itinerary

D. Your badge at an industry conference

E. All of the above

Is the following statement true or false?

Limiting confidential information exposure is not part of your job. It's the job of lawyers, IT security specialists, and uniformed guards.

Apply
Digital Security Basics

CHAPTER 7

Chapter 7 Takeaways

How do you apply digital security basics?

- Protect confidential documents with passwords and encryption, computer networks with firewalls and access controls, and electronic devices with physical security.

- Maintain strong, hard-to-guess passwords.

- Prevent the inflow of unwanted malware with up-to-date antivirus and anti-spyware software.

How Savvy Do You Want to Be?

You have probably studied driving safety basics (driving laws and procedures and basic car mechanics) at some point and taken a driving test to demonstrate you were capable of applying that knowledge on the road. Since then, you have made tens of thousands of split-second decisions about whether to stop as the light turns yellow, change lanes in heavy traffic, double-park for five minutes, take the back way or your usual route, and try to pass a slow vehicle on a narrow two-lane road. You make these decisions almost instinctively and certainly instantaneously. Most of the time, you choose the right course of action because you have learned driving basics. You can maneuver your car safely without knowing everything about your vehicle.

Similarly, digital security basics will help you choose the right course of action as you navigate the information superhighway, making split-second decisions about whether to send an e-mail over a public wireless network, download a document from an unfamiliar Web site, or change a password that you just used while in a hotel conference center lobby. With some familiarity, digital security can also become almost instinctive, allowing you to safely use computing resources without knowing everything about them.

If you are like the majority of corporate citizens, you only need digital security basics because you work in a company where someone else has the corporate functional responsibility for protecting your organization's computing devices, networks, and information. This means that your company's information security department or specialist has already done most, but not all, of the digital security work for you. Perhaps you were provided with a company-issued cell phone, PDA, or laptop that came with some security features turned on or some security programs already loaded. If so, you may have been given some guidelines, documentation, or training describing how to use the technology securely and appropriately.

The remaining responsibility falls on you and is vital to you and your company's information security. If you ignore it or are unaware of it, you might counteract the precautions that were taken in preparing the technology for your secure use. Still, all that is required is to apply the basics even though you may choose to become more technologically savvy. You might want to become familiar with various encryption strengths, identity management systems, data loss prevention content filters, or digital rights management tools. If you are in the IT security group, it is your job function to know about these security technologies. Otherwise, it is your choice.

By analogy, you may be someone who spends days off from work at the auto supply parts store and the wrecking lots looking for spare parts to repair or enhance your car. While this and optional digital security expertise are laudable hobbies, they are not comparable to the kind of digital security savvy I suggest you consider as integral to every employee's job, including your own.

The comparable level of car savvy would include using a seat belt, not just because you will get a ticket if you don't, but because you know it is the safe and sensible thing to do. Comparable car savvy would also include knowing how to change a flat tire and having the equipment to do it. It would include knowing how to check your oil, particularly when your low oil indicator light comes on or knowing to bring your vehicle to a car service station if you do not feel comfortable checking it yourself. If you have this level of car savvy, you are prepared to prevent or get through an emergency situation. If you have to call for assistance, your basic knowledge helps you avoid getting swindled by an unscrupulous mechanic. Your know-how and sense of personal responsibility can make the difference between spending a little on preventative maintenance and spending a fortune to recover from an engine meltdown. If you find yourself on a dark road, in bad weather conditions, in an inhospitable locale, or, worse yet, all three circum-stances at once, your basic knowledge and ability to respond could mean the difference between life and death.

Similarly, applying digital security basics can make the difference between spending a little on prevention or spending a fortune to recover from digital disaster. In the workplace and at home in the twenty-first century, your computer and your online activity can jeopardize your career, financial health, professional reputation, and company fortunes. After all, in cyberspace information is traveling faster than you could possibly drive an automobile, and the rules of the road are constantly changing. You will likely take a wrong turn into a bad cyber neighborhood, and you will probably face the cyber equivalent of car trouble. Following Murphy's Law (if anything can go wrong, it will), it will occur at the worst possible moment under the worst possible circumstances.

Consider, for example, the 2006 Haephrati case, a major computer espionage scandal in Israel's business sector. Malicious code developed by Haephrati was used to control the computers it infected, make changes to their programs, monitor everything they contained, and raid them for information, all without leaving any hint of its existence. The software was sold to three of Israel's largest private investigation companies, which allegedly used it illegally to collect data for their corporate clients, including telecommunications companies, car dealerships, satellite TV providers, and even an office equipment and photocopy company. Police said dozens of companies, which may have included both American and European firms, might have been spied on. Users of the malicious code were targeting competitors, customers, and, in some cases, other divisions within the perpetrator's own company. The malicious code was planted via an e-mail message or a promotional digital media device sent to target companies' employees as though from a well-known and reliable business partner.

The Haephrati case is a remarkable example of twenty-first century intellectual property theft, and it underscores the importance of applying digital security basics. Most employees are not expected to be world-class cyber sleuths capable of detecting sophisticated spying software assimilated into their computer networks by professionals working for their company's competitors. But all employees are expected to keep defensive systems operating and up-to-date on all the computing devices they use or to alert IT security experts when the systems may be faulty or outdated. If you diligently apply the security processes and technologies that your company provides to you, you will reduce cybercrime risks to your company and, in the process, reduce the likelihood of you turning out to be the weak link that a criminal abuses in an effort to steal your company's intellectual property treasures.

All things considered, it is a wise decision to take your computing life at least as seriously as your commuting life. This may mean the cyber equivalent of having jumper cables in your car, knowing the proper water level for your radiator, or choosing to have a really good relationship with a local car mechanic, along with membership in a club that provides emergency roadside services. If you choose the latter for your digital security savvy, you need your IT security administrator to be the digital security equivalent of a local mechanic, and the 24-7 IT help line to provide you emergency roadside service.

While these services are essential, it is doubtful that you can depend solely on your company's IT security resources to implement digital security on all of the devices and software programs you use to develop, transmit, and receive confidential information. Even if you rely on others to change your oil, you need to understand that protecting your car requires periodic oil changes and knowing when to bring in your car for maintenance. Then someone needs to deliver your car to the service station.

The corollary for effective digital security is to recognize when you need help to ensure that digital security technologies are working and to know how to connect your device(s) to your company's digital security service station. In some cases, your company's digital security service station is its network. Maintenance service happens when you connect. In other cases, your company's digital security service station, either in the real or virtual world, requires you to meet in person or in cyberspace with an IT specialist. To work effectively with a digital security mechanic, you will need to know what digital security services you need, how to get them, and from whom.

Digital Security Basics

Digital security basics protect confidential data in digital form and restrict access to the electronic devices and networks that store and transmit it. The following is a list of actions to protect confidential data at rest (stored) and in motion (transmitted). Most companies consider them to be every employee's basic digital security responsibility:

- Limit access to the confidential information you create or share in digital form.
- Keep your passwords strong so they allow only you to access the devices, networks, and information you are authorized to access.
- Physically secure electronic devices.
- Prevent the inflow of malware, such as viruses and spyware.
- Back up any important documents and files that your company does not back up.

Table 5 summarizes the tools you can use to fulfill these responsibilities, and the text that follows explores individual digital security responsibilities in more detail. In the meantime, as you consider the preceding bulleted list and the following table, perhaps you can appreciate that what you need to know about digital security may be much easier to grasp than you ever imagined.

Basic Digital Security Tools	Device Protection	Network Protection	Content Protection
Password-protection: Use security option tools to apply passwords that restrict access to confidential documents.			X
User authentication: Use digital fingerprints or strong passwords to control access to devices, networks, and folders that contain confidential data.	X	X	X
Encryption: Apply company-authorized encryption to confidential files, folders, and drives, for example, USB drives.			X
Secure networks: Use only secure cabled or wireless networks such as virtual private networks (VPNs) configured by your company on your company laptop or PDA; close wireless port(s) when not in use; do not use P2P file sharing or personal instant messages on any device that is used for business; and do not access business information on an uncontrolled device, such as a cyber café computer.	X	X	X
Firewalls: Use firewalls to manage and monitor admittance to networks and electronic devices and to prevent unauthorized access to your network or devices through a connected network.	X	X	X
Antivirus Software: Use antivirus software on all devices that run applications, including removable media such as DVDs and USB drives, and do not open e-mail attachments from unknown sources.	X	X	X

Basic Digital Security Tools *(continued)*	Device Protection	Network Protection	Content Protection
Anti-spyware Software: Use anti-spyware software on all devices that may connect to a network.		X	X
Patches and Updates: Download software patches and updates for operating system and application software.		X	X
Back up: Back up confidential data, and encrypt and securely store the backup media.			X
Permission to download: Download copyrighted materials only with the owner's permission.			X
Physical security: Secure electronic devices (chapter 6), including keeping your laptop, PDA, and cell phone with you and otherwise in a physically secure area when not in use; cable locking your laptop to an immovable object; and locking up removable media, such as USB drives and DVDs, and mobile devices, such as PDAs.	X		X

Table 5

As table 5 indicates, protecting digital devices involves both physical security for the device (chapter 6) and digital or electronic security for data on the device. Network security protects the confidential content accessible through it.

Using a precautionary principle with your technology and being deliberate in your online work can eliminate many risks. Perhaps you have heard the old adages "An ounce of protection is worth a pound of cure" and "Better safe than sorry." Just like taking a breath before revealing information (chapter 5), you can benefit from taking an extra moment to consider the potential impact of your actions before communicating electronically or interacting online.

Advances in hacking, intercepting, and destroying information from electronic devices, such as via infrared from your laptop's wireless port, are proliferating. And tomorrow's new, more dangerous threats will eclipse today's worst cybercrime. While it may be helpful to stay current on specific attack forms, it is more important to understand and apply the digital security basics that build a foundational fortification against all cyber assaults.

Electronic communications and computing technologies are like cars in that they are powerful and potentially hazardous. How well you relate to, handle, and take responsibility for your digital communications and devices will determine whether your powerful assets turn into hazardous liabilities.

Passwords

A password is a form of authentication, which is like a key or a combination unique to the person who possesses it, that opens the door to valuable information.

Password-protecting confidential electronic documents makes it difficult, though not impossible, to open them without the password. Many software applications used to create documents, for example, Microsoft Word/Excel/PowerPoint and Adobe PDF, include tools that allow you to save them as password-protected files, which permit only those who have the password to open or revise them. Unfortunately, a password, unlike your fingerprint, can be misplaced, guessed, forgotten, overheard by an eavesdropper, or stolen. Keeping your password strong and available exclusively to you is essential to digital security.

You create and maintain a strong password by making sure it is

- **At least six characters, including a mix of numbers, letters, and special characters in some combination that is both easy to remember and hard to guess.** "Qt3.14," for example, can be remembered as "Cutie Pi" and the phrase "pearls before swine" can be used to create the password "pearlsB4sw!ne." (As much as you may like these examples, you should never use any password you have seen as an example of a strong password.)

- **Known only to you and not shared or disclosed to anyone under any circumstances.** If you ever have reason to believe that someone other than you has access to your password, you should change it immediately.

- **Hidden, if written down, and encrypted if recorded electronically.** Just as most people will look for a hidden key under the doormat, passwords written on Post-it® notes and placed under keyboards or in desk drawers are easy to find because the hiding places are so obvious.

- **Changed frequently.** Many companies require that network passwords be changed every sixty or ninety days. That is a good interval for changing all your passwords, such as those to your laptop, PDA, mobile phone, and social networking accounts. If changing them frequently causes you to forget them and you are more inclined to write them down, it may be safer to change some of your strong and memorable passwords less frequently. Developing a smart system that works for you is crucial.

- **Entered manually.** Enabling the "save your ID and password" feature on any application may save you time, but it will also save time for any cyber criminal who gets access to your computer or PDA. Also, by entering your password manually, you are more likely to remember it.

These steps are essential to making it difficult for others to guess or steal your password although they do not guarantee your safety from digital danger and damage. Even the strongest passwords may not protect you, your family, or your organization from determined, sophisticated attackers. Still, strong passwords thwart many criminals and force others to use more difficult attack methods.

Encryption

Encryption is an algorithm, sometimes called a cipher, that transforms plain text information into text that is unreadable to anyone except those possessing the decryption (decipher) key. It prevents others from reading your file or your electronic communication even if they can snatch it from your computer or intercept it as it flies through cyberspace. Individual files and folders can be encrypted, as can an entire hard drive.

Encrypting a document provides more protection than simply password-protecting it. And depending on the software application used, password-protecting a document may also encrypt it. If not encrypted, hostile technologies can circumvent passwords and access documents and their content. If a document is encrypted, however, the content is unreadable without the decryption key. Varying types and levels of encryption can be used depending on the security needed for the information and the time allowed for encrypting and decrypting. For instance, the Data Encryption Standard has a 56-bit key but other types of encryption have 128-bit keys or even 256-bit keys, making them more difficult to crack.

Encryption tools are powerful, but if they are not implemented properly, they can create problems just as easily as they can solve them. Using only the encryption technology your company provides allows your company to manage the decryption keys. If you lose yours, you have a backup.

Digital rights management (DRM), and enterprise rights management (ERM), are tools that encrypt documents. Then, applying server-based policies, they prevent the protected content from being decrypted except by specified people or groups, in particular environments, under exact conditions, and for set time periods. Operations such as printing, copying, editing, forwarding, and deleting can be allowed or disallowed for individual pieces of content such as corporate e-mail, documents, and Web pages. Using DRM or ERM technology, you can send a confidential file to one person or a group and be confident it will be accessed and used only as authorized.

Some companies find encryption key management and DRM policy implementation difficult or expensive and do not make them available. If that is the case with your company, you might still take advantage of software offered by your company that includes encryption, such as compressor and archive software. And in any case, you should password-protect confidential documents, which will automatically encrypt them in some applications.

User Authentication

Digital security involves managing access to devices, networks, and confidential content. Your company's IT security group is responsible for access control hardware and software on your company's computing devices, such as its servers, as well as on the corporate networks and the applications, databases, and files on the company's servers and those accessed through your company's network to application service providers on the Internet (referred to as "in the cloud"). Your company's IT security group controls access to computing devices, networks, applications, databases, and files first by defining who is authorized to access them. Access controls are effective if there is some way to authenticate that the person claiming to have permission to access a device, network, application, database, or file is who she claims to be (referred to as identity management). Then digital security technologies can be set to allow in only authorized users and keep out unauthorized individuals.

Authentication is a means of confirming the identity of an authorized user, which might be in the form of a password. For example, to access a computer server or network, a password could be used in combination with a user ID or biometrics, such as a fingerprint scan available as a sign-on to many laptops. Keeping these authentication credentials unique to the user is elemental to an effective identity management system.

Secure Networks

A secure network is one that your company or other trusted organization manages and monitors. If you use only secure wireless networks when transmitting company information from your laptop or PDA, the transmission will be secure whether you are logged on from a steamy cyber café in Mumbai or the VIP lounge of a major metropolitan airport. Check with your company's IT group to see if they have a secure virtual private network (VPN) or use a secure exchange server that allows you to send, receive, and access company information securely over a wired or wireless network from your mobile device.

Public and quasi-public networks, accessed via a network cable or wirelessly, that your company does not own and control pose a significant risk to confidential information. As you sit in a coffee shop, airport terminal, or hotel room (even behind a locked door), accessing a nonsecure network via your mobile device can be equally hazardous and convenient. Public networks allow anyone on them to access open ports, including your computer or mobile device, and to intercept any information you send on the network, including your e-mail.

Consider Tina and Seth's predicament when they were lead consultants in a professional services group, which we'll call "Emmit Corporation." They had three hours between meetings with their customer "Jipp, Inc." to develop presentation materials for Jipp's senior managers. They returned to the lobby of their hotel, which was located close to Jipp's facilities, to find a quiet place to work.

Tina focused her attention on developing the senior management presentation, which summarized a project plan for Jipp's product upgrade based on the priorities and responsibilities discussed during their morning meeting. Seth turned his attention to calculating the costs and defining other terms and conditions for using Emmit's products and services to achieve Jipp's project goals. After an hour, Tina and Seth decided to swap documents so each could review the other's work. Tina sent a copy of her PowerPoint slides to Seth, but before Seth sent his spreadsheet to Tina, she saw she could access his spreadsheet through a peer-to-peer (P2P) network on the shared folder where Seth had saved the file on his laptop.

"I see Seth's Public Folder on My Network Places and can just work on the document there," she told Seth. "Great!" exclaimed Seth. "That makes it a lot easier for us to collaborate on these documents in the short time we have."

Upon returning to Jipp, a senior manager told Tina and Seth that he had received a draft of their presentation and spreadsheet from another Jipp supplier. "Apparently, your competitors were able to easily pick up these documents from the Wi-Fi network in the hotel lobby where you were working on them." Tina and Seth were so stunned and embarrassed that they stammered through their afternoon presentation to Jipp's senior managers, who ultimately decided not to use Emmit for their product upgrade project.

Software tools available over the Internet can sniff out packets of data and intercept e-mails and attachments sent over a public, open Wi-Fi network or wireless hotspot. Snoopers with these tools can easily detect nonsecure Wi-Fi traffic and then collect any passwords and personal information, as well as company confidential information, transmitted via the network. Some operating systems are designed to prompt you with security settings whenever you access a new network, giving you the option to pick a secure wireless network whenever one is available. If you choose a nonsecure network or leave your wireless port on when it is not in use, hackers or aggressive competitors working in the same hotel lobby may gain access to your laptop to look for weaknesses in its security and may access your device or the information on it wirelessly and without your knowledge. To thwart them, you can send e-mail through a secure exchange server or VPN and turn off your wireless capability when you are not actively using it.

If your laptop has shared folders, anyone on a public network, wireless or wired, may be able to access them. You can prevent this by disabling file sharing (in file sharing preferences) before you access a public network. Alternatively, you might set up the shared folders on your laptop with restricted access requiring strong (hard-to-guess) passwords to get into the folders. Encrypting the files in those folders makes them even more secure.

Peer-to-peer file sharing, personal instant messaging, and public computers, such as those in cyber cafés, all create outbound and inbound cyber risks because neither you nor your company controls or secures them. Peer-to-peer file sharing is the exchange of files over a distributed P2P network. Typically, files on the P2P network can be downloaded without the owner uploading them because the files are accessible via a distributed network rather than via a centralized server. As a result, if you use a P2P network, for something as simple as sharing music files with friends, you may unintentionally make confidential documents available on the network. Peer-to-peer file sharing networks also provide a channel for criminals to send and receive malicious software code without your knowing it. You can avoid these perils, as well as illegal copyright violations, if you avoid using P2P file sharing, particularly on any device that you also use for company business.

Likewise, most free, consumer instant messaging (IM) programs provide a channel that is open for your instantaneous communication with friends and family and allows harmful code to be downloaded and installed on your computer. An IM session may permit each user to access the other's hard drives and files, including those containing company confidential information. If you are using an IM program on a computer that has access to your company's network, any malware programs received over the IM channel to your computer can infect your company's entire network. Spyware programs can use IM channels to send commands and download files.

You can avoid these dangers by not using any consumer version of IM on any device that you also use for company business, unless it is an IM program that your company provides to you for business purposes. If your company has provided it to you, it is likely monitored and archived so you will save yourself embarrassment by using it only for company business.

As social networks become more a part of our daily lives, digital security on these networks becomes a greater concern and bigger challenge. Facebook, for example, continues to change its user interface, third-party application requirements, and privacy policies so it can be difficult to know if you are applying the security you want. While some companies make it a policy to not allow employees on social networks during work hours or from computers owned by the company, others require social media engagement for company marketing purposes. In either case, there are opportunities for malicious code to be transferred through these systems and for identities to be compromised. Disabling third-party applications can help secure your account. Turning off Facebook Chat provides additional security because it closes off the instant messaging channel that might otherwise carry malicious code. If social networking is part of your job, your company's IT team can assist you in adjusting settings for maximum security while using social networks from various devices and locations.

As you contemplate digital security basics, it may be helpful to remember that your company's IT department has control over the computing environment in the workplace and you have control over the computing environment in your home and other work settings away from your company's premises. Yet neither you nor your company controls computing environments in the cyber cafés or business centers you will want or are compelled to use while you are on the road, whether for a business trip or a family vacation. These places are equally convenient to cyber criminals and industrial spies as they are to you.

When you are tempted to use a public or quasi-public computer or network, you may have to rely on your knowledge (for example, regarding the reputation of the business center's owner), skills (for example, avoiding opening a confidential e-mail), and instinct to guide you. It is also likely that your company has guidance that you should follow regarding whether and when it is safe for you to use such computing resources.

Firewalls

A firewall is a security technology that serves as a gatekeeper for computers and networks. It inspects network traffic and denies or permits passage based on a set of rules. It endeavors to allow in the good (authorized transmissions) and keep out the bad (unauthorized transmissions). Typically, your company will have one or more firewalls at strategic points, such as at the connection between your company's internal network and the Internet. You also need a personal firewall on your home computer, PDA, cell phone, and laptop if they are outside your company's firewall protection, particularly if they connect remotely to your company's network or if you use them to transmit or receive business or personal information you want to protect.

You might want to verify that the installed firewall is functioning on your laptop, home computer, PDA, or other mobile device and not accidentally deactivated. Without an active firewall preventing malicious code from getting in, any computing device may become infected with hostile software that can destroy data on the device. Your organization becomes vulnerable to that malware if your infected mobile device transmits information to or from your organization's network. No matter how secure it may be, you can bring down your company's entire network after you connect to it without ever knowing that you were the cause.

Preventing the Inflow of Malware: Antivirus, Anti-spyware, and Updates

Every electronic communications or computer technology you use, whether for work or your personal life, including your cell phone and PDA, are potential targets for viruses, spyware, and other malicious programs. Some nasty cyber weapons can jump from one technology to another. Viruses and spyware, for example, can be attached to an e-mail message or embedded in word processing documents, spreadsheets, sound files, or images. They can make their way to your computer, PDA, or cell phone from a trusted Web site or one that is set up specifically to infect Web-surfing visitors. Preventing the inflow of malware, including computer viruses and spyware, is fundamental to digital security.

Computer Virus

A computer virus is a software program that can copy itself and infect a computer without the owner's or user's permission or knowledge. It can destroy your e-mail messages and critical documents, use your computer processor resources, or render your computer useless. It can wipe out every file it encounters on your computer or on your company's network.

You may be seeing signs of a computer virus infection if your computer runs more slowly than normal, stops responding or locks up often, crashes and restarts every few minutes, restarts on its own and then fails to run normally, or if computer applications don't work correctly. Other signs of a virus include your DVD or other drives being inaccessible, your printer not responding to print commands, and your computer showing unusual error messages, distorted menus, or dialog boxes. These incidents might also indicate hardware or software problems that have nothing to do with a virus.

Spyware

In contrast to a computer virus, spyware is software that is installed surreptitiously on a personal computer to secretly monitor the user's behavior, collect various types of personal information (such as passwords), and interfere with the user's control of the computer, like the software used in the Haephrati case. Some spyware is capable of installing additional, unwanted software, redirecting Web browser activity, accessing Web sites that will infect your computer with harmful viruses, and changing computer settings.

Antivirus and Anti-Spyware

Up-to-date antivirus and anti-spyware software running on your computer will significantly reduce your risk of a computer virus or spyware contamination. Company-issued computers and mobile devices will typically include both types of software. If your company has not provided antivirus and anti-spyware software for all of the computing devices that you use and you are obtaining the software yourself, the safest source is the official Web site of your device's operating system, for example, Microsoft or Apple, where you will find information and links to download trustworthy programs. An antivirus or anti-spyware program from an unreliable source may contain a virus or spyware.

In most environments, software updates are downloaded automatically on a schedule. In some cases, you may need to manually download or activate updates by connecting directly to the Web site for the antivirus or anti-spyware software. Some organizations will only update a mobile device such as a laptop when it is connected to a certain network or element of the network within the company.

If you are a perpetual road warrior or a well-ensconced telecommuter who checks your e-mail via the Web, your antivirus and anti-spyware software may not be getting updated frequently enough. Without frequent (generally more than once a month) updates, your computer will be vulnerable to the latest of many thousands of malicious codes.

Some antivirus programs will only scan your computer contents when you turn on your computer. Others will also scan any DVDs and drives that you insert into your computer. If your antivirus software does not scan the files on other media that you connect to your computer nor the individual files that you save to your computer from such media or download from the Internet, it is possible for you to take in a virus without your computer detecting it until the next time you reboot your system. It is probably too late by then. The virus may have already wreaked havoc and the next time you boot up your computer you may see a blue screen with dancing dashes and colons that indicate a virus is destroying your information.

If you still have symptoms of a virus after running up-to-date antivirus software, your computer may have a new virus that antivirus software cannot yet detect or protect against. When in doubt, ask the advice of trained, trusted IT security professionals in your company. It is their job to have current information on viruses, spyware and software patches.

Patches and Updates

While antivirus and anti-spyware software protect against many types of malicious cyber assaults, they do not protect against them all. Cyber criminals have found ways to attack operating systems and applications directly to steal information, snoop on your online activity, and exploit your computer to attack other people's systems. To combat operating system and applications attacks, software owners, including Microsoft, Adobe and Apple, regularly issue security patches and updates. In some IT environments, downloading these patches and updates is done automatically. In your company, you may need to take the initiative or at least be involved enough to follow online prompts about updating and shutting down and rebooting in order for the software fixes to take effect. Either way, you may want to confirm that such patches and updates have been installed.

Antivirus and anti-spyware software, as well as operating system and application security patches and updates, combat outbound and inbound cyber risks, keeping out information or code you do not want and keeping the information integrity that you do want.

Permission to Download

In addition to the risks of using computers and networks that your company does not secure, there is also a risk from using content that your company does not own. It is illegal to copy materials belonging to another person or entity without permission, as tempting and easy as it may be over the Internet. Copyrights, which give the owner exclusive legal rights, exist from the moment original works, such as photographs, graphics, music, text, art, and computer software, are created and fixed in a tangible medium of expression, such as in an electronic document or Web page. The only way to protect yourself and your company from liability for violating copyright laws is to not reproduce, store, download, or transfer, in any form or by any means, copyrighted materials belonging to others unless you have the owner's permission.

Your Judgment

Your company's IT security expert can help ensure that you have the right firewalls, antivirus, anti-spyware, and access controls in place. Still, there are inevitable situations when you may be operating without a safety net, and you will have to rely on your own judgment. What kind of communication would be safe to initiate from the unfamiliar computing environment of a local library in a town that you are visiting? Should you open an e-mail attachment while on the hotel business center computer in order to tweak a sensitive file and then resend it? Who is looking over your shoulder as you type your password? Did you log off completely when you were finished at the cyber café, or could someone backtrack and take over your session after you depart? Is the Wi-Fi network at your sister's home safe enough to send a somewhat sensitive business e-mail? Can you download a technical presentation from a customer's Web site to use as a template for developing a similar presentation for your company?

These are the right, tough questions you should ask yourself whenever you are tempted to work in a computing environment or on a network or with information that neither you nor your company owns or controls. To be safe, avoid using devices, networks, and content that you don't know and trust.

Backing Up Information

Backups are copies of data, files, and applications that can be used to restore lost, corrupted, or accidentally deleted originals. They protect both confidential and nonconfidential information from loss. Hard disk crashes and similar calamities usually happen suddenly with no warning and often at a particularly challenging time, such as in the final stretch of some crucial project. What would you lose if, the next time you turned on your laptop, it did not boot up or it was gone the next time you reached for it? How many days, weeks, or months of work would be lost? How long would it take to recover? To answer these questions, you need to know which important documents and files your company backs up and which it does not. You may also need to know how your computer is backed up and how frequently.

While your company's IT group may back up most of the information that you work with, there is probably some information you need that you are personally responsible for backing up, such as recently created documents saved on your laptop before you leave for a business trip or holiday. If you are working on a critical, time-sensitive project, it may be appropriate to back up your information while you are traveling. You need your own backup strategy to fill in any gaps left by your company's solution. Typically, backups should be done on a

- Daily basis for all indispensable files that you have updated or created that day
- Weekly basis for all of your important file folders and directories
- Monthly basis for your entire hard drive(s)

You won't want to wait for a crash or other mishap where vital information is lost to find out that you should have been backing it up all along.

Once you back up information to a device, such as a portable hard disk, DVD, or USB drive, it should be put in a secure place where you can get to it when it is needed. The backup device or media should be kept separate from what you are backing up, for example, placed in your luggage rather than in your laptop case. Encrypting the backup device's hard drive will secure the confidential information it contains.

Taking Digital Security Basics Home

One perk of empowering yourself as a cyber warrior is that you can bring this knowledge and skill into your own home. Many people do not realize that the digital equivalent of their front and back door-knobs being jiggled every few seconds may be happening on their home computer. Automated programs launched by cyber criminals looking for somewhere to break in can probe home PCs relentlessly. Hackers make this effort, often without caring about the owner's identity, because they want to gain control of a computer so they can use it to launch assaults on other computer systems. Your home computers, even one connected to the Internet only to search the Web, play online games, or send e-mail to friends and family, may be the perfect target because it allows hackers to hide their true location as they initiate attacks, often against high-profile computer systems such as those of government or financial institutions. Once inside your computer, intruders may watch your online activity or cause damage to your computer by reformatting your hard drive or changing your data. If no firewall exists or if password access into your home network or computer is readily guessed, you become an easy target and a likely victim who may never know that your home computer has been compromised. To apply the digital security basics discussed in this chapter to your personal computing devices

- Keep your home PC and other mobile devices that contain confidential or private information in a physically secure location.
- Use a strong password, biometric fingerprint, or other authentication system available to you to restrict access to your computing devices and electronic files.

- Activate and use a personal firewall, such as the ones available on both Windows and Apple operating systems.

- Consider encrypting confidential files and your entire hard drive to protect confidential information at both the file and device level.

- Use antivirus and anti-spyware software and keep them updated.

- Install all security-related patches and updates, which can be downloaded automatically for most operating systems, as well as for many software applications.

- Back up your data and applications onto a medium that you encrypt and keep in a secure location separate from your backed-up devices.

These steps, which provide the digital security basics for your home PC, personal PDA, and mobile digital devices, are especially important if you are going to develop, receive, or access any company-related information on them. While working at home or on the road may help you get more work done, the risk of compromising sensitive company information is too high to justify if you do not apply digital security basics. As soon as you e-mail a file from the company network to your personal e-mail that you later retrieve from home or anywhere else from a browser on the Internet, you may lose the benefit of the entire technical security infrastructure in place at your company. Once outside your company's network and control, information is vulnerable to being accessed, intercepted, corrupted, and misused.

Conversely, you will probably want to use the information technology resources provided by your company for business purposes only. Information security policies in most companies require that you give up any expectation of privacy on company electronic resources.

This means that your company may be monitoring your online activities, including the Web sites you visit and the contents of the e-mail and instant messages that you send and receive. Companies watch network traffic, and some even use spyware to ensure appropriate use of company IT resources.

The Empowering Path to Digital Security

Some people let the fear of technology overwhelm them, though their ignorance is not bliss and often includes the assumption that there is digital security when there is not. Few can be passive bystanders in a digital business world where daily decisions and actions impact digital security. If you are uninformed or unengaged, it is far more likely that you will make a decision that causes you or your company harm.

The wiser path is to apply the empowering digital security basics described in this chapter. By protecting your own and your company's information, you avoid cyber catastrophe and the frustration, embarrassment, inefficiency, and injury caused by information loss. As you become savvier, you will discover which security technologies are used to protect the equipment you have been issued, such as your cell phone, PDA, and laptop, and the software applications they run. You may find that, despite its resources, your company is not taking care of all your digital security needs. You may have to do something to update or activate the security features and programs configured into your company-issued technology. Understanding digital security basics will help you to know what digital security services you require from your company's IT security professionals and what preventative measures are left to you.

The best (and easiest for many people) time to learn about digital security is when learning to use a new technology. What do you need to do to keep confidential information from going out unintentionally and prevent malicious code from entering your new device or application? Using table 5 as your checklist and your company's IT security group as a central digital security supplier and mechanic, it should be easy to stay current, consistent, and comprehensive in applying digital security basics to all your electronic communications and computing applications and devices.

Accepting the responsibility for applying digital security basics will also help you in your personal life because it is likely that you use electronic devices to access, store, and work with your personal information. Digital security basics help you create safeguards on any device or network that you use.

Prepare to Need Help and Hope You Never Will

One of the most powerful weapons in your arsenal of cyber self-defense is the one that you can construct yourself from a simple online document or sheet of paper. Consider taking a few moments now rather than when you are in a desperate rush and panic to write down the telephone numbers for your company's IT support personnel, names and version numbers of the applications you use, software license numbers, and serial numbers for the technological devices on which you depend.

When something goes wrong, you will need this information, and it will help to have it all in one place. Appendix C, "Contacts for Information Protection Help," offers a place to develop your emergency help numbers list. If you use it, keep this book or a copy of appendix C with you in your briefcase or wallet or in a Web-accessible file—perhaps a password-protected or encrypted attachment to an e-mail you send to your personal e-mail account—that is apart from any of your devices. Someday, it may save you from digital devastation.

Chapter 7 Spot Quiz
Apply Digital Security Basics

(The answer key can be found in appendix D)

Which of the following security technologies best secures the contents of your laptop if it is stolen?

A. Encrypted hard disk

B. Strong password

C. Cable lock

D. Global positioning system

E. Desktop firewall

Is the following statement true or false?

As long as I am not logged on to the Internet from a wireless network, no one can access my laptop via its wireless port.

Construct
the Appropriate
Precautionary Force Field

CHAPTER 8

Chapter 8 Takeaways

How do you construct an appropriate precautionary force field?

- Employ together and use consistently five baseline confidential information protections: NDAs, limited disclosures, confidentiality notices, digital controls, and physical security.

- Strengthen safeguards for more sensitive information and circumstances that create higher than typical loss risks.

- Use informed good judgment and seek guidance from your company's policies, classifications, and information protection experts.

The Force Fields You Know

You create personal precautionary force fields every day when you lock your front door and turn a light on when leaving your home for the evening or when you put your cash in your wallet, which you then put into your pocket or purse. If asked about it, you might attribute these actions to common sense, instinct, or internalized habit. Other choices, such as deciding to take an umbrella and wear a raincoat to work after hearing that rain is predicted, are conscious and may be based on a thoughtful, though brief, analysis.

To create your personal precautionary force fields, you adroitly assess risks and make complex choices, sometimes automatically. If you drive a car, you pay attention to where you park it and lock the doors to reduce the risk of theft when you leave it on a city street. If it is an expensive car, you have probably invested in an electronic alarm system and possibly in a steering wheel lock.

If you have a dog, you make certain that its collar has a tag engraved with your telephone number, and you bring a leash on your walks. Perhaps without even realizing it, you have analyzed the risk of losing your dog or getting a fine. If you have children, you make sure they are supervised when they are in a pool, and you have them take swimming lessons. You balance your concern for their safety with their need for independence as you create a precautionary force field for their well-being. In each dimension of your life, there is some automatic and hard-wired or thoughtfully considered set of actions that you take, or avoid taking, to create precautionary force fields around yourself, those you love (children, pets), your tangible (home, money, car), and intangible (your reputation) treasures.

Your personal force field is a model for protecting valuable company information and private data. Both your personal and your company information force fields require analyzing the risks, understanding the basic protection options, and applying appropriate safeguards based on the circumstances. Both are made strong with exercise and use, and both are easy, particularly when they become second nature.

The Analogous Information Protection Force Field

Just as personal protection force fields are based on some external requirements (stopping your car at a red flashing traffic signal) and some internal decisions (choosing a well-lit street over a dark alley), information protection force fields also come from external requirements (your company's information protection policy) and internal decisions (applying judgment to a specific situation where the policy is silent). The more comfortable you are with assessing information risks and applying the right protections, the more likely it is that you will erect appropriate precautionary force fields. The goal is to internalize sensitivity for protecting information just as you internalize sensitivity for protecting your loved ones and the material things you value. Applying the appropriate force fields then becomes second nature.

The Information Age's lightning speed advances present many potential perils to our professional and personal lives. It behooves everyone in the workforce to quickly become attuned to when information protection force fields are needed and to learn to create them almost automatically. The following questions provide an easy filter to help determine if a precautionary force field is even needed:

- Does the situation involve confidential information? If not then you will not need a precautionary force field to protect it (though you might want one to protect the integrity and availability of nonconfidential information).

- Do you need to reveal the confidential information in this circumstance? If not, then avoiding disclosure may also circumvent the need for a precautionary force field.

One mistake many people make is that, once they decide they need to divulge some information, they open the floodgates. Their information sharing becomes unfettered, unnecessary, and reckless. A person's need to receive some information is not a license for her to receive anything and everything she wants (chapter 5). Confidential information disclosure should be limited to only the information required by the specific recipient to do something that will aid the information owner.

If you do not have to make known the confidential information you work with, then your job is to protect the information from being exposed to a hacker, eavesdropper, or other unintended recipient. If you *do* need to make known certain confidential information, then your job is to ensure that it reaches only the intended recipients. A precautionary force field enables such restrained sharing and helps to shrink vulnerabilities by inducing intended recipients to protect the information that you make available to them.

Giving Instructions with Your Gift of Information

Have you ever given a friend a flowering plant and then noticed it dead or thrown away a few weeks later? If the plant did not come with instructions on how to take care of it, it is likely that your friend did not know that it should be watered only once every two weeks and kept in direct sunlight. If the plant does come with clear instructions and perhaps a packet of plant food, it is much more likely that your friend will take care of it. In the same way, when you give information, it may also lose its confidentiality, or be shared inappropriately, if you do not provide instructions and possibly resources for its ongoing protection.

Most recipients of confidential information are, like you, busy and bombarded with demands for their attention. They may also feel conflicting pulls. Their egos may be boosted if they share the information you shared with them, or they may be able to wield some power if they publicize the new ideas. It is your responsibility to protect the confidential information you develop and use in your own environment, as well as to do what you can to make sure that those with whom you share it will protect it in theirs. To be effective, everyone who is authorized to have the shielded information, regardless of their profession and association, must sustain the precautionary force field. Your clear instructions to a recipient about how to maintain the information's precautionary force field helps to ensure the force field's effectiveness.

Constructing a Precautionary Force Field

It is easy to build a precautionary force field if you start with the understanding that there is a baseline, or minimum protection level, that should be applied to all confidential information. The flowering potted plant will live if you give it water once every two weeks and keep it in direct sunlight. That is the baseline. As master gardeners know, plantscaping is both an art and a science. You can go well beyond this baseline and feed the plant nutrients, trim the plant at a particular time and in a particular way, and talk to it regularly to make it thrive. You may decide that the expensive potted orchid deserves an investment in a monthly orchid food feeding, but it is not worth your time to give it daily words of encouragement. Knowing the baseline that ensures the plant will live makes it straightforward for you to balance the costs and benefits of your additional options, above and beyond the baseline level.

In the same way, knowing the information protection baseline that will sustain confidentiality should make it easy for you to balance the costs and benefits of your additional protection options.

The Five Baseline Information Protection Elements

The five baseline elements of a precautionary force field for information protection are

- Contractual obligations via an NDA or similarly binding agreement prior to disclosure (chapter 4)

- Confidential information disclosure limitations, based on your need to reveal it (chapter 5)

- Notification (verbal, physical, and electronic) that the information is confidential (chapter 4)

- Digital controls that limit access to your electronic devices, files, and electronic communications (chapter 7)

- Physical security to safeguard work areas and limit confidential information exposure (chapter 6)

These five baseline elements must be applied together to form a precautionary force field. They represent the minimum information protection requirements. They are like water and sunlight for a flowering plant in that no one element is sufficient. A plant must have both to survive, and much more to thrive.

A client took me on a tour of the cockpit for its $850,000 integrated badge, keycard, and closed-circuit television system that monitored the company's manufacturing facilities. As impressive as the state-of-the-art system was, the company's investment was literally thrown to the wind because several employees regularly propped open the back door to the manufacturing and test laboratory, which allowed anyone, with or without a badge or keycard, to enter the company's facilities. The opened door rendered the expensive keycard and monitoring system useless because it could not determine, based on badges or keycards, who was in the company's facilities.

Establishing the precautionary force field baseline requires a conscious and concerted effort to ensure that no essential element is missing or left open. If it is, it can render all other existing protections ineffective.

At times, it will be clear to you, based on your company's policies or a directive from your manager, exactly what you should do to apply each of the precautionary force field baseline elements in a particular situation. Other times, it will be up to you to use your informed good judgment. In either case, the process will be trouble-free if you understand the five core information protection elements listed earlier, which form the building blocks of your precautionary force field.

Increasing and Decreasing the Precautionary Force Field's Strength

You strengthen the force field, which you will want to do if the information's sensitivity or the circumstances call for it, by strengthening one or more of the five baseline elements. Adding strength is easy, although determining the appropriate precaution level requires some discernment. It requires balancing protection costs and the potential inconvenience against all the benefits, including preserving valuable company secrets, establishing and maintaining a reputation for strong intellectual property protection, and avoiding a big future inconvenience, embarrassment, or loss if the information is compromised. Answers to two questions will help determine a precautionary force field's appropriate strength:

- How sensitive is the information?
- What risks of loss are created by the circumstances?

More sensitive information and riskier circumstances require stronger precautionary measures. Less familiar recipients and less trusted information delivery methods create a higher risk and a need for stronger safeguards. For example, if the intended recipient works in an underdeveloped country and must be sent the information via a nonsecure network, or if the information must be disseminated broadly, more protections may be necessary compared to instances when only a few known individuals will have access to information that is sent over a secure network. Table 6 depicts how three levels of a precautionary force field can be designed based on information's sensitivity and its circumstantial loss risk. As indicated in the table key, level 1 represents the information protection baseline, level 2 represents a strengthening of one or more of each of the baseline's information protection elements, and level 3 represents a precautionary force field with the strongest information protection elements compared to level 1 or level 2.

Protection Levels Based on Sensitivity and Risk		
	Very Sensitive Information	Less Sensitive Information
High-risk circumstances	Level 3 information protections	Level 2 information protections
Low-risk circumstances	Level 3 or level 2 information protections	Level 1 information protections
Key: Baseline information protections = Level 1 Stronger protections =Level 2 Strongest protections =Level 3		

Table 6

The following table shows how you might adapt the five baseline infor-mation protection elements to increase the precautionary force field's baseline level 1 protections to establish two progressively stronger information protection levels.

Force Field Elements	Contractual Obligations	Limited Disclosures	Notification/ Instructions	Digital Controls	Physical Security
Force Field Elements Applied to Three Protection Levels					
Protection Level 1	Least stringent contract terms	Disclose what may be useful to a specific project	Use confidenti-ality notices	Password-restrict access	Store in a secure facility
Protection Level 2	Moderate protection requirements	Disclose only what is reasonably needed for a specific task	Use confi-dentiality notices and provide written confidentiality instructions	Apply encryption to transmit	Store only in a secure, restricted access area
Protection Level 3	Stringent protection requirements and individual information user sign-off required	Disclose only what is essezntial (as little as possible)	Use confiden-tiality notices and provide in-person, individual confidentiality instruction (training)	Apply encryption to store or transmit	Isolate all physical embodiments in a secure, access-controlled area

Table 7

Generally, a stronger force field requires more effort, more investment, and more inconvenience than a weaker force field. Strengthening every force field element is not always better. If the benefits from adding protections outweigh the costs of creating a stronger force field, all you may need to do is increase the strength of one or two of the five core elements.

Contractual Obligations

As described in chapter 4, a binding confidentiality agreement, typically called a nondisclosure agreement or NDA, should be in place before confidential information is disclosed. The NDA establishes the recipient's obligation to protect the shared information in a legally enforceable contract. Without an NDA, you can only hope that the person to whom you are revealing company secrets will protect them. As with each element of the precautionary force field, the NDA can be strengthened from its base level to include more rigorous obligations.

Some NDAs require, for example, that the confidential information recipient protects the disclosing company's information in the same manner as the receiving company protects its own sensitive information. What if the disclosing company is a high-tech manufacturing company and the receiving company is its janitorial service provider? It is possible that the janitorial service provider applies only very weak information protections to its own sensitive information. There is a continuum of options for strengthening such an NDA—from requiring that the janitorial firm take at least reasonable measures to protect the technology company's information to requiring that the janitorial firm allow only select long-term employees to clean certain sections of the manufacturing company's facilities. The latter may be appropriate for reaching level 3 or level 2 protections in the previous tables.

Another option, as indicated in table 7, is to require individual employees to sign off on the NDA terms. Many of my clients have opted for this mechanism to strengthen their NDAs: they require that each individual in the contractor firm sign a confirmation that he understands his obligations under the NDA between his employer (for example, the janitorial services company) and the contracting company (for example, the technology manufacturer). One client, a telecommunications company, hired an engineering firm to do contract work. There was an NDA between the telecommunications company and the engineering firm, but there was uncertainty about the individual engineers' understanding of their obligations under that NDA. My firm developed a Contractor Rules & Requirements (CR&Rs) document to supplement and strengthen the NDA. The telecommunications company now uses the CR&Rs document to instruct each engineer employed by the contractor firm to protect the telecommunications company's information. The NDA between the telecommunications and engineering firms is strengthened by requiring that each engineer have instructions and sign an acknowledgement that he understands the instructions for protecting the telecommunications company's information.

While changing NDA terms or requiring individual contractor sign-off to such terms may be outside your job purview, understanding that these options are available to strengthen a force field probably is not. Whenever you intend to share confidential information, you can contribute to its value by being aware of and suggesting appropriate precautionary force field tailoring.

Limited Disclosures

As described in chapter 5, a core precautionary force field element is to limit the information you reveal and to whom you reveal it. If the information is highly sensitive and you need to disclose it to an unfamiliar new supplier in Romania where you have few professional contacts, you will want to be careful to divulge only the very specific information that the supplier needs. You should then use the other precautionary force field elements to ensure the supplier limits its disclosure of your company's information to those individuals at the supplier company who need and will use the information to benefit your company. For this limitation on the supplier's disclosure to be enforceable, it should be clearly stated in the NDA.

One frequently used method of limiting confidential information disclosure is to segment a project so no one individual or firm has access to all of the component pieces that would make known the secrets of the entire project. I have worked with many software companies to establish business processes for distributing source code among software engineers in such a way that no one of them and no outsourced software engineering company would have enough of it to threaten the entire project.

Disclosures can be limited by scope, as in the example of breaking up source code, or by level of detail. If you are a sales associate and a prospective employee on a job interview at your firm asks how you maintain relationships with customers, you might tell her that you use a contact database that helps you determine when it is time to call a customer and you follow up with either an e-mail or a telephone call, depending on the prospect. You probably would not need to tell her that you have 2,147 active contacts, of which you call on approximately twenty-five in any given week, and your top five priority contacts are IBM, Xerox, HP, Sony, and Dell, because each of these companies has purchased more than $1 million in equipment from your company.

Receiving confidential information is a burden, particularly when there is an NDA in place that imposes obligations on the recipient for protecting the information received. By limiting information disclosure based on your need to reveal, you limit the burden on the recipient. "I could tell you, but then I'd have to kill you" (a line spoken by Tom Cruise in *Top Gun*) is an extreme expression of this burden. The reverse is more apt: "I will tell you only what you need to know so as to not encumber you with undue protection obligations." Limiting confidential information disclosure is particularly effective when paired with notification: "I'm providing you with the competitive analysis section of our marketing plan, which is the only section you will need to help us with our project. Because each section of our marketing plan is confidential, I won't bother you with what you don't need to know so you don't have the added load of protecting that information too."

Confidentiality Notification and Instructions

Chapter 4 describes in detail the verbal, physical, and electronic alerts you can use to notify a recipient that information is confidential. Confidentiality notices in your precautionary force field should reflect the sensitivity of the information and take into account the disclosure circumstances. If you are discussing a new site layout with a colleague in the facilities department and the two of you are sketching rough design plans on a whiteboard, it may be sufficient to remind your colleague verbally that your discussion is confidential.

On the other hand, when you bring in a group of customers to train them on how to use new machinery, you may need significant confidentiality message reinforcements. After determining that one of its customers leaked confidential information learned from a training session, a company asked my firm to help find ways for them to reinforce the confidentiality of their machine tools designs, processes, and know-how. By implementing my recommendations, they took advantage of many opportunities to shower their customers with confidentiality messages during their visits to my client's premises, particularly for training:

- A banner across the internal training room door now reads "Confidential Customer Training: Confidential Tooling."
- The binder covers for the training material includes a conspicuous confidentiality notice.
- In the training binder, behind a tab labeled "confidentiality," we provide an explanation of how confidentiality protects our client's competitive advantages and how that benefits the customer and which training materials are confidential with specific instructions for protecting them.
- The trainer begins the training session by describing the materials in the binder that include the company's confidential information and instructions for protecting it.
- The trainer reinforces the confidentiality message, including how confidentiality benefits the customer, before each break and at the end of each training session.
- Each lavatory stall has one of our firm's information protection awareness–raising bulletins taped to the inside wall.
- A curtain surrounds the tooling equipment itself. When the curtain is opened for the training, it includes a neon sign that blinks the word "confidential."

These measures were inexpensive to implement, and the potential benefits far outweigh the costs. Information protection notifications and instructions are often a creative and particularly cost-effective precautionary force field building block.

Digital Controls

As described in chapter 7, digital security is achieved by restricting access to electronic information—whether at rest—in the form of messages, documents or files stored on your laptop computer, a company server, a USB drive, or on your mobile phone—or in motion—being transmitted over a wired or wireless network. If you work for a company that employs more than a few people, it is likely that IT experts helped set up your company-issued computer, your company's wired and wireless networks, and its servers and facilities to meet your company's digital security standards. It is your job to avail yourself of the technologies and processes offered by your IT group and to ensure you do not weaken their effectiveness.

As with the other four core elements of your precautionary force field, you have options for strengthening digital security, such as the following for information stored on your laptop:

- Password required to boot up
- Biometric, for example, fingerprint, identifier required to boot up
- A screen saver that requires a password to resume work
- Password-protected documents
- Password-protected folders (with passwords that are different from those used to open the documents) to hold the password-protected documents
- Encrypted documents and folders
- Encrypted hard drives

The controls listed above may be implemented independently or in any combination. Options for strengthening digital security or other force field elements are not mutually exclusive.

Some options, such as encrypting private information stored on a laptop or other mobile device, may be required by your company or by law. If a hard drive containing private information is not encrypted and it is lost or stolen, privacy laws may obligate your company to report the loss to all of the private information owners.

Several encryption strengths are available. The stronger the encryption, the harder it is to crack. Stronger encryption costs more, however, and may be more difficult to manage; in addition, it may not be globally usable without an export license. As with the other core protections in your force field, increasing base level digital security is a judgment call. You or an IT expert in your organization will need to decide whether encryption is needed and under what circumstances you should apply which available encryption strength.

Physical Security

As described in chapter 6, physical security reduces confidential information exposure, particularly in your work areas. It is risky to leave papers scattered all over your desk when you depart from work, but even more so if the information is highly sensitive and if your desk is temporarily located in a customer's facility where your company's competitors may also have desks. If you work with highly sensitive information, you should lock away its physical embodiments, regardless of the format, when you are not at your desk. You might also use a cable to lock your laptop to your desk, even if the contents are encrypted, if the risks of theft are high, which they are in many places, including, possibly, your own cubicle. Highly sensitive information, such as information classified as "Company Confidential: Special Handling," can be protected with layers of physical security, including keeping hard copies of documents in a locked filing cabinet in a locked office in an access-restricted, monitored building.

As the previous examples illustrate, there are many options for strengthening each of the five baseline elements and the overall force field. Some of these options may be required by your company's policies or by contracts or laws that impose confidentiality obligations on your company and you. In many cases, there are additional opportunities for you to use your creativity and informed good judgment to determine the appropriate force field strength and the options that may be used to create it.

Processes and Workflows

While it may seem like common sense to apply the five baseline protections to the confidential information you develop and share, other pulls on your attention can distract you from implementing them consistently, particularly if you have to think about how to construct the appropriate force field each time you develop or share sensitive information. Establishing a precautionary force field requires a bit of effort, time, and consideration. You and your company can reduce all of these by integrating precautionary force fields into business processes and workflows so that protecting information is part of how you do your work, not an added duty.

If you are a researcher in a pharmaceutical company, for example, and you oversee your company's clinical trials for new products, you will want to have a standard process in place for ensuring the physicians and patients involved in those clinical trials protect the confidential information they develop or receive. Once you determine the appropriate information precautions for physicians and patients in current clinical trials (ensuring that all participants sign NDAs and receive confidentiality instructions, only the information they need, and resources for physical and digital security), the process can be made standard for all future clinical trials. By establishing standardized, integrated information protection processes, you narrow the number of situations where you will need to make decisions. You leverage the effort, time, and consideration it may take to construct a suitable information protection force field by applying it to all similar circumstances. Thoughtfully constructed precautionary force fields then become standard practice, not an afterthought.

The Force Field and Classifications

Information classifications can both identify confidential information sensitivity levels and provide a shorthand for the type of precautionary force field that users should apply to the information. For example, the protection levels in tables 6 and 7 might correspond to the following classifications:

Classifications and Corresponding Protection Levels	
Protection Level	**Classification**
Level 1	Company Confidential
Level 2	Company Confidential: Private
Level 3	Company Confidential: Special Handling

Table 8

The classification indicates a need to apply baseline protections and to strengthen these safeguards for information classified at higher levels. The level 2 (Company Confidential: Private) and level 3 (Company Confidential: Special Handling) classifications are subsets of level 1 (Company Confidential) information. All levels must be protected with at least the baseline precautionary force field.

Classifications can help determine how to protect the information, not only on a case-by-case basis, but also on a predetermined type-by-type or situation-by-situation basis. For example, all information classified as "Company Confidential: Private" will generally require encryption, particularly before transmission outside your company's secure network.

The following table describes employee protection responsibilities associated with each confidential information classification based on best practices.

Classifications and Corresponding Employee Responsibilities

Classifications	Employee Responsibilities Summary
Company Confidential	− Label conspicuously with the classification. − Ensure all recipients are notified and reminded of confidentiality. − Limit disclosures based on each recipient's need to know. − Require a signed NDA before disclosing to any company outsider. − Safeguard work areas at the company and other facilities. − Store to avoid casual observation. − Dispose in a secure manner and based on retention schedules. − Control access to computing resources using approved access control software. − Secure electronic communications with passwords. − Obtain management authorization before publicly disclosing information that may, with other publicly available information, reveal confidential information. − Report any suspected improper disclosure or access and any inadequate protection. − Apply informed good judgment to ensure protection.

Company Confidential: Private	– **All protections for "Company Confidential" information and:**
	– Disclose only with the owner's permission.
	– Access only the specific information that is needed.
	– Limit disclosure, distribution, and access to only those with a specific need to know.
	– Encrypt all versions that are stored on a mobile device or transmitted electronically.
	– Keep in a locked, secure area.
	– Send hard copies or electronic media with an outer envelope marked "To be opened by addressee only."
Company Confidential: Special Handling	– **All protections for "Company Confidential" information and:**
	– Obtain authorization from the originator or responsible manager before accessing, copying, or further distributing.
	– Limit disclosure, distribution, and access based on a substantial business need to know, and reveal only the specific information that is needed.
	– Encrypt all electronically stored and transmitted versions.
	– Originator should apply rights management or document control to record and track each copy's distribution, use, and destruction.
	– Keep in a locked, secure area.
	– Send hard copies or electronic media with an outer envelope marked "To be opened by addressee only."

Table 9

Fulfilling employee responsibilities associated with each classification contributes to creating precautionary force fields that are appropriate to information sensitivity levels.

Informed Good Judgment

Company policies and guidelines such as those in table 9 may direct you to apply baseline (or more) protections to meet information classification procedure requirements or to address specific situations. But a comprehensive information protection guidebook would have to be voluminous to describe all information loss risks, as well as the diverse and numerous types and degrees of protections that might reduce those risks. If such a tome were compiled, it would be too unwieldy to be useful. The moment it was published, it would be outdated. Continuous advancements in technologies and our ever-changing business environment perpetually create new information loss risks. Adapting to them will likely require relying on your informed good judgment to tailor precautionary force fields.

A primary goal of this book is to help you to develop a sixth sense and internal filter (chapters 5 and 6) that triggers an alert when a precautionary force field seems insufficient. Under such conditions, you will need to remedy the situation or ask your manager or other responsible individual, such as an IT or corporate security or legal specialist, to help fix the information protection inadequacy.

When you are creating or improving a precautionary force field to protect confidential information, you should always start by applying the five baseline force field elements:

- NDAs
- Disclosure limits
- Confidentiality notifications

- Digital controls
- Physical security

Then you can add suitable creative options to reinforce and strengthen each element. Whether you need to add or intensify options to strengthen your protection baseline will depend on the information's sensitivity level and the circumstances that produce its exposure risks. If the information is highly sensitive or the disclosure circumstances create a high information loss risk (you reveal sensitive information to an independent consultant who is simultaneously working for a competitor), you will want to tailor increased security measures beyond the baseline elements to address those risks.

In most cases, someone in your company with the corporate functional responsibility for establishing information protection systems will determine your organization's overall information protection strategy. She will ensure that there are firewalls and other technologies to restrict access to the company's networks. She will decide how strong your passwords need to be or if some biometric identifier, for example, a fingerprint or retinal scan, is required. She may put monitoring systems in place using software on your company's network and closed-circuit TV cameras in your company's buildings. If you are holding a highly confidential meeting in a conference room, however, it may be your decision to have the conference room scanned for recording equipment in advance of the meeting, to ban cell phones because most include recorders and cameras, or to prohibit use of adjacent offices during your meeting.

If you are alert to the kinds of options that are available for safeguarding information, you can enjoy the creative challenge of using these options to upgrade precautionary force fields. The Coca-Cola secret formula legend is that only three people know the formula, it is kept in a safe, and it takes two people together to assemble the safe's combination. If your company is in the food, beverage, pharmaceutical, or chemical production industry, it may also have a secret recipe, formula, or ingredient that should be similarly protected, and you may have an opportunity to establish a precautionary force field similar to the one developed by Coca-Cola.

If you are a software developer and a prospective customer wants to review your source code, you might enhance its precautionary force field by inserting some oddities in the code that do not belong there, such as a love poem. If your company ever suspects that its code was copied illegally, you could help establish proof by finding your love poem in the copied code. Adding distinctly unnecessary code is a precautionary force field option that has worked well for many companies, although in at least one case a creative software engineer included profanities in the source code, which offended his company's software reviewers.

While embellishing force fields for formulas and source code may be outside your job scope, it is likely that you construct precautionary force fields by applying a combination of company mandates and your creativity on a daily basis. If you were to need financial analysis assistance, for example, you might ask a consultant with a great reputation for analytics to send you a proposal. You might decide that he needs a spreadsheet with your company's projected costs and revenues for three products in order to develop his proposal. Because it is your job to apply a precautionary force field for the information you plan to disclose, you begin by requiring that the consultant sign an NDA (a company mandate). To limit disclosure, you might remove spreadsheet fields that are unnecessary for the consultant's purposes or replace the data in those fields with random lists of names (a creative option based on your informed good judgment). In addition to marking the spreadsheet "[Company Name] Confidential" (another company mandate), you might reinforce the copyright and confidentiality notice by stating in your cover e-mail that those notices must remain on the spreadsheet and on any copies of it (a creative option based on your informed good judgment). You password-protect the spreadsheet to prevent an unauthorized recipient from opening the electronic document (a company mandate). You might creatively comply with your company's confidentiality notice mandate by talking to the consultant about his confidentiality responsibilities. You might ask him to confirm that his laptop, which will receive the confidential spreadsheet, is encrypted or otherwise secure. How does he keep it safe when he travels? You remind him to not forward the confidential spreadsheet to anyone, and you review with the consultant what he should say if a competitor asks about any work he is doing for your firm (all based on your informed good judgment). Finally, if the consultant's proposal is not accepted, you request that he destroy his copy of the spreadsheet (a company mandate). By taking these steps before and after sending the spreadsheet to the consultant, you establish a customized precautionary force field by combining company mandates and your creative, thoughtful enhancements.

In the course of your daily work, whenever you are sharing or making confidential information accessible, you can take a deep breath to activate your innate risk mitigation expertise (your inner guide for determining appropriate information safeguards to address specific information risk circumstances). You might start by comparing any existing protections to the five baseline elements. If your company has adopted information classifications, you should use them to make your work easier by assessing the protection threshold suitable to the information's classification.

You do not need to be familiar with every information protection option. The five baseline precautionary force field components are sufficient to protect most confidential information sharing. Once the baseline is in place, you can upgrade any or all force field elements using familiar and resourceful protection options that will suit the circumstances.

Ultimately, these processes for protecting information, creating force fields, and strengthening them as appropriate, will be fully integrated into your day-to-day workflow. With practice, applying precautionary force fields to protect confidential information becomes second nature in the same way you intuitively apply precautions in other dimensions of your daily life, for your home, money, health, loved ones, and reputation. In all these realms, avoiding loss and buying peace of mind is well worth the effort.

Chapter 8 Spot Quiz
Applying the Appropriate Precautionary Force Field

(The answer key can be found in appendix D)

Which of the following activities or technologies strengthens a precautionary force field but is not one of the baseline confidential information protection elements?

A. Securing your work area

B. Encrypting highly confidential materials before communicating them via the Internet

C. Utilizing digital rights management

D. Ensuring the recipient knows the information is confidential

E. All of the above

Is the following statement true or false?

Obtaining a signed NDA from the recipient of confidential information is not enough. You must determine that the recipient has a real need to know the information before you share it. You must also remind the recipient that the information is confidential and she is obligated to protect it.

Fulfill
Confidentiality Obligations
to Others

CHAPTER 9

Chapter 9 Takeaways

What are your confidentiality obligations to others?

- Protect and use only as you are authorized
  - your organization's confidential information
  - information others entrust to your organization subject to nondisclosure obligations
  - personally identifiable information that your company collects from individuals
- Use another company's confidential information only after receiving permission.

The Contract between Your Employer and You

If you are like most people reading this book, you probably signed an NDA or other agreement that included confidentiality provisions when you started working for your employer. You probably don't remember exactly what it specifies, other than that it requires you to protect confidential information. Perhaps, like most people, when you signed the agreement, you thought you would meet your responsibilities under it if you applied your common sense. After reading to this point, you likely understand that it takes more than common sense to protect confidential information. Applying the ten steps described in this book can be easy, but it is not innate knowledge.

Are you able to locate your contract with your employer? It is worth the effort to get a copy so you can review it now that you understand more about protecting confidential information. After all, the NDA you signed is a commitment that you made to your employer. It is also a document that can be used to fire you, fine you, and put you in jail if you violate its terms. While NDAs differ from one another, the following provisions are fairly standard ones from an employee confidentiality agreement that several of my clients use:

> Confidential Information includes not only information disclosed by the Company to you in the course of employment, but also information developed or learned by you, and information received from third parties under a duty of confidentiality, during the course of your employment with the Company ... You agree at all times to hold all Confidential Information in strict confidence and to not disclose, use, copy, publish, summarize, or remove from the premises of the Company any Confidential Information, except as necessary to carry out your assigned responsibilities as a Company employee.

What does it mean to hold information in "strict confidence ... except as necessary" to fulfill your job function? The International Association for Standardization defines confidentiality as "ensuring that information is accessible only to those authorized to have access." Applying this definition, one could argue that you are obligated to limit your own use and disclosure of company confidential information as well as to ensure it is accessible through you only to those individuals who are authorized by your company to have it.

I hope that, at this point, you are having an "aha" moment as you realize that everything you have read in this book will help you meet your NDA obligations to protect information *and* contribute more value to your company because there are compelling reasons for protecting information that go beyond merely complying with the NDA you signed.

Even if you did not sign an NDA, the obligation to protect your employer's assets, including its information, is generally implied by law. Under common law (case law), every employee has a duty to protect company confidential information and trade secrets. The Winklevoss twins' claim that Facebook founder Zuckerberg misappropriated Harvard Connection's trade secrets (chapter 4) would have to be based on common law, assuming Zuckerberg never signed an NDA.

In the contractual provisions quoted earlier, as in most employee NDAs, the obligation to keep confidential information in strict confidence applies not only to your company's confidential information (disclosed to, developed by, or learned by you), but also to any "information received from third parties under a duty of confidentiality." The purpose of extending your obligation to information received from third parties is to ensure that your company can meet its confidentiality obligations to others through you.

Your Company Is Obligated to Protect Personal Information

Almost every business collects personal information from individuals, including customers and employees. E-commerce, Web-based communities, social networks, frequent buyer programs, store savings cards, and online financial transactions increase the amount of personal information a firm accumulates. Dozens of state, federal, and international privacy laws require organizations to protect personally-identifying information. Failure to comply with these laws can result in fines, imprisonment, or both.

What is personal or private information? One federal statute defines nonpublic personal information as information resulting from any transaction with a consumer, such as a customer's name and address. Some state statutes requiring that lost personal data be reported define personal information as first name or first initial and last name tied to a Social Security number, driver's license, or an account, credit, or debit card number and password. A European Union regulation defines personal data as any information relating to an identified or identifiable natural person. Your company probably took many of these definitions into account when defining a private information classification, such as the one discussed in chapter 4. All definitions share a common theme: Personal information identifies something unique about an individual, which, if exposed, would threaten that person's anonymity.

Technology widens the scope of information that is personally identifying. In 2006, the United States government asked Google, Yahoo, and America Online (AOL) to disclose information about their customers' Internet searches. Each company attempted to mask any personally identifiable information, yet one reporter was able to determine where users lived and what health conditions they experienced. While the data did not include individual names, it did contain user IP addresses (Internet Protocol numbers assigned to each point of contact on the Internet) and search queries, such as addresses entered to get directions and illness terms used to research medical treatments. Information that did not seem personal ultimately revealed very private information.

As a result, companies are under increasing pressure to destroy rather than keep information that could be used to discover personal information. For a company like Google, particularly after buying

DoubleClick, an online advertising company, there is tremendous value in holding onto their records from their very first days as a search engine. They show which users were searching for what types of products or services, such as the IP addresses for the 3,572,000 individuals who searched for low-calorie diet dog food and the 5,069,000 individuals who searched for multi-line telephone equipment, over the last several years. While such metadata provides insights helpful to companies that want to target their advertising to sell dog food or telephone equipment, it also may divulge private information. The fact that you or your company has access to such information does not entitle you to exploit or even keep it.

In the wrong hands, personal information can be used to invade an individual's privacy or commit identity theft or fraud. Someone with another's personal information could withdraw money from her bank account or apply for a credit card in her name and use it without authorization. Privacy regulations impose obligations on companies to protect individuals from such losses and other unauthorized personal information uses.

As discussed in chapter 3, U.S. as well as international laws, which are increasingly relevant in our global business environment, impose obligations on your company to protect their citizens' personal information.

As you might imagine, these laws differ, although there are common themes. The Organization for Economic Cooperation and Development issued guidelines in 1980 addressing the privacy of personal records, with the express purpose of setting standards for government privacy rules. These guidelines are the underpinnings of most national and international laws. The following summarizes the two privacy guidelines that are most relevant to you:

- Collecting personal data should be limited, consented to by the data owner, and used only for specified purposes.

- Personal data should be protected by reasonable security safeguards against risk of loss or unauthorized access, use, or disclosure.

There are other requirements common to many privacy laws that privacy professionals, IT security specialists, and lawyers in your company can implement. The two requirements enumerated above can only be achieved by your company with your active participation, which is generally expected no matter your other job responsibilities.

What is required of you? First, you should request or obtain personal information from or about another individual only if it is for a legitimate purpose (and you use it only for that purpose) and the person consents to giving you the information. Emergency room workers at Martin Memorial Medical Center in Stuart, Florida, faced the consequences of violating this principle after they took photographs of kite surfer Stephen Howard Schafer's mauled body from his February 3, 2010, shark attack.

Second, you should apply an appropriate precautionary force field (chapter 8) to the personal information that your company collects. This includes encrypting personal information before you store it on a mobile device or transmit it. Many privacy laws require organizations that lose personal information to notify those individuals affected by such losses if the information was not encrypted. If you encrypt the electronic device on which you store personal information about individuals and it is lost or stolen, your company's duty to report the loss to the information owners may not be triggered.

More recently, however, state laws, such as those enacted in Massachusetts and Nevada, impose an affirmative obligation on businesses to encrypt all electronic transmissions (except facsimiles) of a customer's personal information if the information is sent outside the business' secure system. Consequently, encrypting all transmissions, as well as personal information stored on mobile devices, ensures compliance with these regulations.

Learning from Others' Mistakes

A company I will call "Cavgroup Oil & Gas" approved a proposal to implement new compensation, benefits, and stock options plans for its employees. Kathy, Cavgroup's compensation director, worked with one of the country's premier compensation consulting firms, "Insight," to develop the recommended plans. Kathy hired Insight to help apply the plans to Cavgroup's nine thousand employees because Insight had the software tools needed to develop a fully fleshed out salary and benefits schedule. After putting Cavgroup's employee data into Insight's database, Insight could conduct analyses at their local offices, which were in another state, rather than traveling to Cavgroup's headquarters.

Insight's team leader, Henry, copied every Cavgroup employee's company identification number, Social Security number, and salary and benefits history onto a DVD before leaving Cavgroup's offices for the weekend. Monday morning, upon returning to his office, Henry realized he had left the DVD with the Cavgroup employee information on an airplane. Henry was so upset that he waited two weeks to report the missing DVD to his boss. After hearing the bad news, Henry's boss worked for days to develop a strategy for dealing with the lost DVD and delayed reporting the incident to Cavgroup officials for another three days.

Cavgroup's executive management team was stunned. Because the information on the lost DVD was not encrypted, Cavgroup was required by law to notify in writing all of its nine thousand employees that their personal information may have been compromised. Cavgroup also had to purchase a credit monitoring service to catch security or credit violations directed against any of its employees by an identity thief who might have gotten hold of the DVD. Both companies' reputations were seriously tarnished from bad publicity surrounding the incident, including the reporting delay. Cavgroup fired Insight and contemplated taking legal action against them. Insight lost a year's worth of profitable work as a consequence. Henry lost his job and continues to carry guilt and shame for causing his company and its client such an embarrassing loss.

If Henry had established the appropriate precautionary force field, he might have avoided his job dismissal and the guilt and shame associated with being careless. The Cavgroup incident also teaches us that waiting to report personal information losses may increase the harm caused by them, including theft and negative publicity. To help an organization meet its obligations to protect personal information, every employee is responsible for limiting the collection and use of others' personal information, ensuring adequate protection, including encryption, and immediately reporting any lost personal information.

Your Company Is Obligated by Contract to Protect Third-party Information

In contrast to the personal information your firm receives from individuals, most of the information your company receives from other companies is subject to an NDA or a purchase, collaboration, or trading partner agreement with confidentiality terms. These contracts obligate your company to protect the confidential information entrusted to it. In many cases, the agreements specify how the information should be treated. Some confidentiality obligations are general. Their fulfillment depends on the standards of the company that receives the confidential information. For example, "Recipient will protect the disclosing company's confidential information with the same degree of care it applies to protect its own confidential information, but in no case with less than reasonable care." If your company were to sign a contract with a supplier that includes such a provision, your company—and you by extension—would be obligated to apply at least the same level of protection to the supplier's confidential information as you apply to your own company's confidential information.

Confidentiality provisions may also be significantly more stringent. Many companies impose very strict, detailed information protection obligations on their suppliers and other business partners. An agreement may specify the individuals or groups in your company who are authorized to receive the business partner's confidential information.

It may require that those individuals who access partner information electronically use multi-factor authentication, and it may require your company to track the information as it is used and disseminated.

Some companies and many government agencies are well-known for having rigorous auditing procedures to ensure their suppliers meet their information protection obligations. These audits will take up less of your company's time and may ultimately be deemed unnecessary if you are conscientious about fulfilling your company's commitment to protecting others' information.

If you are unfamiliar with the obligations imposed on your company, you should review the confidentiality provisions of any contracts between your company and its customers, suppliers, business partners, and contractors with whom you work. Without such familiarity, you might breach your company's legal obligations to others as well as your confidentiality obligations to your employer.

Consider the lessons that can be learned from Orit, a manufacturing manager for "Ability Appliance," who worked directly with "Handevice Grips" to integrate their grip aid components into Ability's appliances. Ability executives abruptly terminated their relationship with Handevice because of the recent worldwide financial crisis. Within days of receiving the contract termination notice, Handevice's attorney wrote to Ability's general counsel, Nanci, indicating that all confidential materials received by Handevice from Ability were returned or destroyed. "Please let me know when to expect Ability's return of Handevice's confidential materials and confirmation that electronic copies have been destroyed, as required by our contract," wrote the attorney.

Nanci asked Orit to return all of Handevice's confidential materials, which Nanci had verified was required by the contract between Ability and Handevice. Orit was aghast and told Nanci that her department had not kept track of the confidential materials received from Handevice. She did not know how to retrieve copies that her department members may have given to customers and prospects and to manufacturing and marketing consultants. "Besides," she told Nanci, "a lot of the confidential information we shared with Handevice we shared verbally. They could not have returned that to us."

Orit's team had told Handevice everything about Ability's plans to attach Handevice's grip devices to Ability's appliance products, as well as their manufacturing and marketing strategies. Had Orit been familiar with the NDA requirement to confirm verbal confidential disclosures in writing, she and others at Ability may not have discussed as much as they did with Handevice. They assumed, as many do, that the NDA covered all of their discussions.

Having just reviewed Ability's contract with Handevice, Nanci knew it required that any confidential information disclosed verbally had to be confirmed as confidential in writing within thirty days or it would not be subject to the NDA. Ability's failure to send Handevice any such written statements resulted in Ability's confidentiality loss. Handevice was free to use or further disclose the verbally-revealed information.

Orit's failure to keep track of Handevice's confidential information throughout the business relationship made it impossible for Ability to return confidential materials and thereby comply with the contract. After a business relationship terminates is not the time to begin to understand contractually required separation procedures. It is too late by then.

Handevice sued Ability and won an award of consequential damages from Ability for its breach of contract. The amount awarded exceeded Ability's anticipated savings from terminating the Handevice contract. The lesson from Ability, Orit, and Nanci is to become familiar with contract terms related to confidentiality at the beginning of a business relationship, both to avoid violating legal obligations and to provide an important customer service by meeting requirements to protect information entrusted by others to your company.

Your Obligation to Yourself: Avoid a Trade Secret Lawsuit

Failure to protect your company's confidential information is almost certainly a violation of your legal obligation to your company. Failure to protect confidential information that other companies entrust to your company likely violates contracts that exist between them. Failure to protect personal information that belongs to consumers or other individuals, including fellow employees, probably violates privacy laws that apply to your company. Last, but not least, failure to keep yourself out of a court proceeding targeting you violates your responsibility to protect yourself from an expensive, messy, time-consuming lawsuit. You owe it to yourself to steer clear of the distraction, career derailment, legal fees, and court fines (potentially hundreds of thousands of dollars), and to avert a mandatory stay in a state or federal penitentiary.

Protecting confidential information helps you meet these self-preservation responsibilities. If you treat company confidential information as a form of intellectual property, and you only access, disclose, make available, or use it as you are authorized, you will avoid trade secret law violations and their adverse consequences. Laws criminalizing trade secret theft are found in many international jurisdictions, including the United States, Europe, and Japan. The Uniform Trade Secrets Act (UTSA), used as a model for most state trade secrets laws in the United States, prohibits disclosing or using a company's trade secrets without the owner's consent. The Economic Espionage Act (EEA), a federal criminal statute in the United States, prohibits trade secret theft, unauthorized trade secret disclosure or use, and the receipt of stolen trade secrets.

Caryn Camp learned about these laws the hard way when she worked for IDEXX Laboratories, Inc., a leading manufacturer of veterinary diagnostic tests, kits, and software. When she began working as an entry-level manufacturing chemist in 1995, she signed an NDA, a Noncompete Agreement, and IDEXX's Corporate Policy on Ethics in Business Conduct, all of which clearly defined her obligation to protect IDEXX's confidential information and not to disclose or use it for her own or another's benefit.

When Camp was searching for a new job three years later, she e-mailed her résumé to Stephen Martin, a veterinarian and owner of an enterprise that aspired to compete with IDEXX. Martin's flattering and friendly correspondence to Camp eventually included requests for IDEXX manufacturing process instructions, internal IDEXX operating procedures, copies of laboratory notebook pages, customer lists, internal company e-mails, and IDEXX test kits. Camp sent Martin the information and documents he requested, perhaps in response to his e-mailed propositions that his company would give her "enough bonus money to buy your own house for cash. Maybe on the lake." He emphasized that her continued good work might result in her becoming a CEO at a company he influenced. Camp knew she was a spy. In an e-mail to Martin she wrote, "Aren't I awful? I'm liking this spy business way too much." She obviously liked it enough to risk her promising career, her reputation, her personal freedoms, and her hard-earned salary and savings.

On the day she quit IDEXX, Camp wrote an e-mail message to Martin letting him know that he could expect a final batch of information from her that would make him "feel like a kid on Christmas Day." Perhaps it was the stress or excitement of leaving IDEXX that caused her to send this e-mail to IDEXX's head of global marketing in error. IDEXX notified the U.S. Attorney, and Camp and Martin were tried and convicted under the EEA of conspiring to steal IDEXX trade secrets. Camp pled guilty and, in exchange for a plea bargain to testify against Martin, was sentenced in late 1999 to three years of probation, $7,500 restitution, and a $1,500 special assessment. Martin was sentenced to 366 days of imprisonment, three years of supervised release, $7,500 in restitution, and $800 in a special assessment. They were fortunate. Penalties associated with a conviction under the EEA can include up to $500,000 in fines and fifteen years in federal prison.

The incidental damages to one's career, reputation, and life path may be even more devastating.

Meeting your information protection duty to yourself, and thereby avoiding these undesirable consequences, is easy if you distinguish confidential from nonconfidential information (chapters 3 and 4), know who is authorized to have and use confidential information (chapter 5), and apply the appropriate precautions to protect confidential information (chapters 6–8). If you, like Camp, are ever tempted to deviate from your moral compass, it may be helpful to remind yourself of this duty and the clear course of action to get back on track. Fulfilling your information protection responsibilities is a straightforward route to preclude stealing trade secrets. The challenge occurs when there is confusion about which of the company's information is trade secret, the circumstances under which it should be revealed or used, and the appropriate level of precaution that should be applied to protect it. If you ignore your confusion now, it will likely arise later in conflict. Lack of clarity about what is confidential and the responsibilities for protecting it becomes apparent most often when an employee leaves (or, as in the case of Caryn Camp, considers leaving) one company for another. The probable consequences are threats, lawsuits, legal fees, and distraction from your current or potential job. To avoid undesirable outcomes later, consider redoubling your efforts now to be attentive to what your company owns and to make sure you protect confidentiality and do not inadvertently disclose, use, or take trade secrets illegally.

For anyone leaving or considering leaving an employer, it is essential to know what information can be used lawfully with a new employer.

If you carefully abstain from taking confidential information, which your current employer may define very broadly, in most cases you will be free to use the general skills and knowledge you acquire while working for your current employer in any future employment. Trade secrets are distinguishable from general skill and knowledge in that trade secrets involve applying skill and knowledge to specific company circumstances.

To illustrate, if you are a sales associate and you learned how to use a customer relationship management (CRM) system while working for your current employer, you can take that general skill with you to your next employer. Familiarity with a commercially available CRM program's functionality is not a trade secret. On the other hand, information about how your employer customized the CRM system, why changes were implemented, at what cost, in what timeframe, and with what result may all be considered confidential information owned by your current employer. Understanding these distinctions now may prevent costly disagreements later. Your manager or someone in your company's legal department will want to help you avoid misunderstandings about company confidential information and trade secrets, particularly if you may be leaving the company. Asking for their help now may avert a painful dispute later.

Other Companies' Trade Secrets

The same laws, penalties, and consequences of stealing your employer's trade secrets apply to the theft of other companies' trade secrets. Just as confusion adds to the likelihood that you might inadvertently misuse your employer's trade secrets, confusion adds to the likelihood that you might inadvertently steal another company's trade secrets. If you are working with a customer and she says she can give you a copy of the confidential proposal she received from one of your competitors, should you accept it? If you are interviewing a job candidate who offers to provide you with confidential materials he developed for his current employer, should you review them? A vendor tells you that you are not the only one who came to his company asking about titanium parts. Your competitor has asked as well. The vendor recommends that you take a copy of the proposal his company recently put together for your competitor. How should you respond? The answer is, in almost all cases, "No, thank you." Passing up opportunities to accept gifts of or steal others' confidential information deflects trouble.

If there is confusion as to whether the information offered may be confidential or whether the person offering it is authorized to provide it, your manager or someone in your company's legal department will want to help you determine if you are safe in accepting the offered material. The question is complex, and how you respond can have significant consequences, including a messy, expensive, reputation-diminishing disagreement or lawsuit.

Suppose you are in the chewing gum business, and you have been working with a packaging designer for many years. One day, the designer asks if he can make a suggestion for a great new product line. Before you can answer, he describes his idea, "People love their designer coffees and tea. I think you should make coffee-flavored chewing gums to match the varieties of coffees and organic herbal chewing gums to match the most popular brands of herbal tea. Youth from twelve to eighteen are buying these kinds of things like crazy. Just think of your marketing tag line, 'No need to wait for the water to boil.'" Your company has been looking for some fresh ideas, and this seems to be a good one. At your request, your company develops the new product line, and it is wildly successful.

Is your heart pounding with anxiety from this story? Perhaps it should be. It is likely that the package designer who put forward his suggestion will come knocking on your company's literal or proverbial door and demand, "Either pay me a royalty on the coffee- and tea-flavored gum, or I will see to it that you cannot sell that product line at all."

How can someone with an idea and no development, production, or sales costs expect a royalty based on his idea? How can information freely given be charged for down the road? How can your company be liable for using information that was not subject to an NDA? To answer these questions fully, we would have to look at the contract between the packaging designer and your company in the scenario above. We might also look at patents issued to the packaging designer for coffee- and tea-flavored chewing gum. Rather than going into an explanation about why and how these things matter, it is more important to make two important points. First, there is a real danger to accepting unsolicited product ideas from non-company employees (chapter 4). Second, the best way to avoid the danger is to follow your company's procedures for receiving such proposals. The procedures will likely include requiring the person who wants to make a suggestion sign an agreement before making new ideas known to your company. That way, your company has a chance to negotiate the terms in advance of using the offered ideas rather than being threatened in the future.

Protecting information is a two-way street. Not only does it require protecting sensitive information from going out to the wrong recipient, it also requires shielding you and your company from the potential jeopardy of incoming information. Your obligation to your company and to yourself requires vigilance in both directions.

Mistakes Are Easy in Today's Hurried, Technology-enabled World

In chapter 5, I describe how technology makes it easy to reveal confidential information to unintended recipients. While these mistakes can have dire consequences that cause your company embarrassment and lost competitive value, they are even more disastrous when dealing with information owned by customers, business partners, and other stakeholders who entrust their confidential information to your company.

A client, whom I will call "IndustriaPipe," experienced an unfortunate calamity caused by a simple mistake. Mary, an employee, was responsible for developing two bids. The first was to send a prospective customer a proposal for a closed-circuit television (CCTV) video inspection system for their sanitation piping. The second was to provide an existing customer with a proposal for licensing IndustriaPipe's pipeline inspection software. The bid to the existing customer had to be sent by Thursday to meet the Friday request for proposal (RFP) deadline. Although there was no deadline for the prospect's CCTV proposal, Mary wanted to send it out by Thursday as well in order to maintain momentum in their sales cycle. On Thursday afternoon, Mary rushed to finalize the bid proposals in time to get them in the overnight mail pickup. After printing both proposals, she gave them a final review and put each into one of the overnight delivery envelopes she had prepared.

On Friday, Mary tracked both packages online and confirmed that IndustriaPipe's prospect and its customer received their respective items. She was shocked to learn the following week that the customer had received a package from her that did not include a response to their RFP. Mary had put the customer's proposal in the envelope prepared for the prospect and vice versa. By the time she realized her mistake, the customer had closed the bid process so IndustriaPipe lost its opportunity to be considered for the contract. The customer was also upset to see the bid for the CCTV system, intended for IndustriaPipe's prospect, because it proposed selling a new CCTV system at a lower price than what the customer had paid the year before. The prospect decided against buying the CCTV system from IndustriaPipe because, after receiving another company's confidential information from Mary, the prospect was concerned that IndustriaPipe could not protect its confidential information.

Mary's mistake cost IndustriaPipe a contract with its customer, including any ongoing maintenance fees, a new business relationship with its prospect, and potential liability and diminished reputation from revealing, in error, its own, its customer's, and its prospect's confidential information. IndustriaPipe estimates the cost of Mary's error at more than $500,000.

One way to avoid such costly mistakes is to be particularly cautious before you send any confidential information, whether it belongs to your employer, its customers, prospects, or business partners, and whether it is sent physically or electronically. At IndustriaPipe, all bid proposals must now be developed and sent at separate times to avoid mixing up one for another when they are put into an overnight mail envelope or attached to an e-mail message.

What precautions do you need to take, particularly in situations of stress, fatigue, or distraction, to avoid costly mistakes, save business relationships, and maintain a positive reputation? Many errors that result in lost confidentiality can be prevented by anticipating when stress or technology increases their likelihood.

Meeting Obligations, Creating Trust

While protecting information is essential to your own and your company's success for numerous reasons, none is more striking than the impact it has on trust—between you and your company; between your company and its partners; and among you, your company, and your company's customers. Your own and your company's attention to protecting information creates trust. Your company's partners and customers are more likely to want to work with your firm if it demonstrates its ability to protect its own competitive advantage, as well as the valuable information entrusted to it. Rather than getting in the way of business, protecting customer and partner information enables business success by laying the foundation for trusting relationships.

One of my clients, whom I will call "EDA, Co.," is a well-known provider of electronic design automation tools used primarily to create printed circuit boards. My client's customers are computer equipment manufacturers, such as IBM, Samsung, and Hewlett-Packard. To be effective, EDA's engineers need to work directly with its customers' engineers. Customer information, including customers' detailed unreleased product designs, has to be available on EDA's computer network so EDA can assist with customer design development. How could EDA's customers trust EDA with their most sensitive information, knowing that EDA is also working side by side with their fiercest competitors?

The customers imposed tough information protection obligations on EDA. Some customers required isolating computer servers; others required identifying specific EDA employees to work with their information. Still others required creating unique physical security safeguards for their magnetic tapes. EDA could have been overwhelmed with complying with these differing obligations to protect their customers' information. Instead, EDA called my firm to help them implement a customer information protection strategy that incorporated its customers' most stringent information protections. EDA even built a research and development facility with state-of-the-art physical and electronic security for the sole purpose of working with its customers.

These efforts resulted in customers trusting that EDA was able to protect their confidential information and keep it from migrating through EDA to a competitor. And, because the information protection strategy that EDA offensively adopted was as strong as the most demanding customers' information protection requirements, all customers viewed EDA's information protection as a value-added service. EDA promoted this service with prospective new customers and discovered that its ability to provide intellectual property protection assurances gave it a significant marketing advantage, which built the foundation for EDA's profitable customer relationships and market leadership position.

Another of my clients, a leading pharmaceutical company, had a different reason for establishing trust through a robust information protection program. The company, referred to here as Antacid, Inc., saw an opportunity to develop a blockbuster antacid drug. To do so, however, they had to partner with their biggest rival, another leading pharmaceutical company. Entering into a joint venture with a formidable competitor, sometimes called "coopetition," necessitates both companies to clearly define the confidential information they bring to the partnership, and both must include information protections in the processes and technologies they use to work together.

Most important, all employees working on the project must actively and intelligently protect their own company's and the other organization's confidential information. More than an NDA is required for coopetition (or any collaboration) to work. To inspire confidence and success in such a venture, everyone involved must participate in creating a positively confidential setting. In the case of Antacid, Inc., their information protection strategy based on these principles enabled the coopetition partners to jointly develop and share in the profits from what became the most profitable antacid on the market.

Could your company, like EDA or Antacid, Inc., gain from an information protection strategy that would give your company's business partners, customers, and prospects confidence in your ability to protect their information and intellectual property? Doing more than what is required by contractual confidentiality obligations builds a reputation for attentive intellectual asset protection, which creates trust and increases your company's value proposition.

Chapter 9 Spot Quiz
Fulfill Confidentiality Obligations To Others

(The answer key can be found in appendix D)

Which of the following circumstances could lead to a tarnished reputation, a decline in sales, and criminal prosecution for you or your company?

A. Failing to adequately protect the confidential information and other intellectual property entrusted to your company by its business partners

B. Integrating, adapting, or building upon the intellectual property of other individuals or companies without proper authorization, whether intentionally or inadvertently

C. Keeping detailed customer or employee personal and private information

D. All of the above

Is the following statement true or false?

There is no danger in using a product idea suggested by a contractor in casual conversation.

Support Your Company's Information Protection Ecosystem

Chapter 10 Takeaways

How do you support your company's information protection ecosystem?

- Activate your sixth sense so you discern when something seems amiss and might cause information loss or compromise; trust your instincts to be curious.

- Look for opportunities to improve your company's information protection.

- Report information vulnerabilities.

- Be an advocate with your colleagues, reminding them that everyone benefits from a positively confidential corporate culture.

Activating a Sixth Sense

You become attuned to opportunities to preserve or enhance confidential information's value and to help avoid situations that would diminish that value by cultivating an information protection sixth sense or internal filter (chapters 5, 6, and 8). Your sixth sense should be triggered, for example, when a printing contractor offers to show you materials printed for a competitor if you are willing to pay the contractor a little extra cash under the table. In this case, red flashing lights and sirens should go off inside your mind, letting you know that your print contractor is not trustworthy with confidential information. He may be offering your competitor a similar deal to get your company's secrets.

What if you see someone you do not know in the photocopy room near your work area at eleven o'clock at night making photocopies of hundreds of documents? When you say hello, he is so startled that he jumps with a look of terror on his face, quickly picks up all the documents, and leaves hastily. Again, your sixth sense should trigger (blaring) alarm bells. The goal, however, is for you to have a sixth sense that intuits potential trouble even when it is much less obvious.

The Cuckoo's Egg: Tracking a Spy through the Maze of Computer Espionage, a classic text on cybercrime investigation, is Clifford Stoll's first-person account of his pursuit of a hacker who penetrated the computers of Lawrence Berkeley National Laboratory. Stoll's adventure started when he investigated a seventy-five-cent accounting discrepancy. That single, simple query led to the revelation that many millions of dollars worth of information was in danger of being stolen and exploited. The long trail led to Germany and Eastern Europe and involved the NSA, CIA, FBI, and United States Air Force. It uncovered a hacker who had been selling the information he came across to the KGB (the Soviet Union's national security agency from 1954 until 1991). And it all began with curiosity about a seventy-five-cent accounting discrepancy.

One of the most important lessons in this legendary (and true) story is that if you allow your sixth sense to trigger your curiosity about any suspicious activity, even if it seems minor, it may result in the discovery of otherwise undetected incidents or long-term activities that could annihilate your company if they are not stopped. You will be most effective at protecting information if you activate your sixth sense and follow your curiosity.

Information Protection Change Agent

Your enterprise is an ecosystem that changes as you change. As you shift your attention by taking action to protect confidential information, you influence the attention and actions of your colleagues, which transforms the corporate culture.

Tara, a manager at a client company I will call "SpinFilters," learned this soon after receiving some very good news. SpinFilters' senior vice president of engineering called Tara to congratulate her. "It's still very secret, but I have decided that you will be leading a new project team to develop your polypropylene tube invention." After years of hard work and long hours developing her invention, the news was Tara's dream come true. Tara left her cubicle so excited that she thought she was going to burst. She headed for the break room for a cup of tea to calm her nerves.

Several of Tara's colleagues greeted her and asked, "What's new?" Tara realized she had to respond quickly without revealing her secret news. It is difficult to know the problems Tara might have caused by telling her colleagues then that she would be leading a new project team. Their feelings might have been hurt, and the surprise announcement might have fueled rumors and misinformation. Because the break room is a semi-public space, people that Tara did not see and whom she would not want to know the news might have overheard her. It is often in a company's best interests to control the timing and wording of an important announcement to mitigate possible negative reactions and consequences.

Tara told her colleagues, "I've been thinking about how important it is for us to protect SpinFilters' sensitive information. If our competitors learned about what we are doing, it would be devastating. Our open culture and the cubicles we work in are great for collaboration and innovation, but sometimes pose a challenge to protecting what we create. It's good we are required to review information protection policies once a year and attend some information protection training, but sometimes I think we need to discuss specifically how to balance SpinFilters' interests in both sharing and protecting sensitive information."

Tom, a fellow engineer, disagreed, telling Tara it was common sense to protect sensitive information. Shoshanna found common ground by saying, "Even common sense can evade us when we are in a hurry or inconvenienced by taking an extra step to safeguard information. We always have so many other things on our minds. I've overheard many sensitive conversations in the cubicles I pass by as I bring our vendors to our conference rooms. I've often wished I had reminded everyone to be careful about what they say when I know that outsiders will be visiting our facility."

Tara was successful in engaging her colleagues in a useful dialogue about the importance of protecting information and specific ways to reduce exposing it to loss. With her nerves calmed, Tara returned to her cubicle to work on the polypropylene tube project.

After SpinFilters' formal announcement that Tara was leading the new project, she shared with me that her cover-up conversation about protecting information helped create a better work environment. Aware employees actively safeguarding confidential information made SpinFilters a safer place to share more freely with customers and business partners. Tara often used topics related to protecting information, such as how to create strong passwords, when to use NDAs, and how to apply encryption, to engage colleagues in dialogue anytime she was at a loss for a good conversation starter. This was especially helpful for Tara to avoid revealing the secret of her exciting new project while catching up with colleagues before a meeting began, having lunch with a co-worker, or taking a break at the water cooler.

Intention, attention, attitude, and behavior, such as Tara's initiating a discussion about protecting information when she was excitedly wanting to announce her big news, strengthen a company's entire information protection ecosystem and become part of the organization's culture. The positively confidential corporate culture forms a safe container where the business' intangible underpinnings are secure, which enables the company to take advantage of opportunities to share (or not) ideas and information for its optimal advantage.

Advocacy and Leadership

Like Tara, you can advocate for and lead improvement by using every information exchange as a teaching opportunity, suggesting ways to reduce visible information loss risks, and being a role model for protecting information. Each time you share or receive confidential information, you have an opening to remind those who are privy to it that the information is confidential (chapter 4), the steps to take to protect the information (chapter 8), and the reasons why protecting information helps everyone involved (chapter 1).

Taking advantage of these everyday opportunities to teach others to protect information ensures that your work colleagues, such as your teammate in the cubicle down the hall, the consultant you just hired, and the prospective vendor you spoke to at lunch, will not be the people who destroy your company by revealing what you shared with them in hoped-for confidence. Quick and easy reminders can make a lasting impact on the hearts, minds, and behaviors of those to whom you expose confidential information.

Another occasion for advocacy and leadership is any perceived instance of potential information loss. If you attend a trade show, for example, and overhear others discussing your organization's unreleased product, you might

- Ask the people talking to be more discreet. To minimize feeling embarrassed or shy, remind yourself that you are doing your colleagues a favor by asking them to avoid unnecessary confidential information exposures. One thoughtful reminder will often eliminate the immediate problem.

- Report the problem, exposure, or policy violation to an information protection professional in your company. Some departments, for example, IT security, corporate security, and compliance, are responsible for directing organization-wide confidential information protection. By letting an expert who works in one of those departments know that you witnessed a potential problem, the expert can more fully understand and address it. While the incident may be an isolated, inadvertent failure to share confidential information with discretion, it may also indicate a more widespread deficiency.

- Suggest remedial actions that will reduce the likelihood of similar vulnerabilities in the future. If the individuals who discussed your company's unreleased products are fellow employees, you might suggest to their manager or the information protection specialist in your company that employees should be trained to be discreet before they attend any future industry trade shows.

Key to being an effective advocate and leader is being a role model. You can gain credibility quickly if you consistently protect confidential information. When you talk the talk by speaking out for information protection and then walk the walk by visibly applying information protection measures, others will follow. You become a catalyst and a leader of a positively confidential organization. You inspire others by helping them to understand the benefits to themselves and their company of their vigilant participation in safeguarding information. You bring about a corporate culture comprising individuals who respect and protect confidential information, which, in turn, boosts individual and organizational achievement. By modeling and inspiring information protection improvement, you help yourself and others to meet the challenges and opportunities of preserving confidentiality in a continuously changing business world.

Tell and Show That You Care about Protecting Information

The best catalyst for changing a company's information protection ecosystem is success. One clear sign of success is when customers trust and buy from a company because it has a corporate culture that protects information. The more your company's customers and business partners are confident that your company will protect their confidential and private information, the safer they will feel about sharing it. You acquire and build stronger business relationships by telling customers and business partners—and showing them through your actions—that you respect and protect their information's confidentiality (chapter 9). If they feel safe, they share higher quality information, which allows your company to better respond to their needs and increases your company's sales, market share, and profits.

As you interact with prospects and customers and discover incidents where they are lax in protecting their own information, you also have an opportunity to recommend information safeguard improvements. Your suggestions add a valuable service enhancement and positively differentiate you and your company to your customer or prospect. If a customer sends you an RFP that is not marked confidential or if it does not explicitly describe how information about the project should be protected, for example, you might send an e-mail letting that customer know that your company takes confidential information protection seriously and, although their RFP did not address the subject, your company will protect the customer's confidential information, including the RFP contents.

Helping customers and business partners protect their information builds strong company-customer trust and relationships.

Report Improper Disclosures and Opportunities to Improve Information Protection

Your company's information ecosystem is a delicate balance of people, technology, business processes, relationships, laws, and incentives to share and protect information. The ecosystem is changing constantly, as its elements change, as your company's competitive landscape changes, as technologies change, as new legislation is adopted and enforced, and as the world is transformed. The tension between your company's interests in sharing and protecting information continuously shifts. The technologies and tools that enable accessing and protecting information revolutionize what is possible for both.

Sustaining a comprehensive and effective information protection strategy tailored to your company's needs is no small task. For most successful companies, it takes a team of representatives from the legal, IT, compliance, human resources, privacy and security departments working together. Your advocacy and information protection leadership will support the specialists charged with overseeing your company's information protection strategy, and it will aid your company as a whole.

If your company has not clearly identified whom to contact when you need help protecting information or where to report an information exposure or loss incident, you might ask a representative from your legal, IT, or security department to recommend someone. The referral may depend on the nature of the help you need or the incident you want to report. In all cases, your request for help and your incident reports (of potential or actual information loss or compromise) will assist those responsible for ensuring that the legal, technical, physical, and practical aspects of your company's information protection strategy are properly implemented. The effectiveness of those who are responsible for overseeing your company's confidential information protection depends on your active engagement, which makes those who are responsible for oversight eager to help you do what is right.

Conversely, failing to report incidents or to advocate for information protection implementation can be devastating to you, your company, and those individuals with information protection oversight responsibilities. Consider Anu's experience at a company I will call "Balm Inc." After a week of conducting customer focus groups for its new Balmstick product, Anu returned to her office to compile and analyze the data. The Balmstick was developed to counter a competitor's recent launch of a similar product. Anu knew Balm's product development and launch would have to be completed quickly to compete effectively and regain some critical market share.

On Monday morning, Anu was frustrated that it took an unusually long time to boot up and run her computer. She was anxious to complete her data analysis, so she rebooted. When that did not fix the problem, she figured she just had a slow network connection and forged ahead. On Tuesday, when Anu arrived at work, she was surprised to find that her keyboard was sticky and the notes she had left on her desk were out of order. She made a disparaging comment about the janitorial staff and then got right to work. On Wednesday, when Anu returned from lunch, her computer screen showed an error message stating that the password entered was invalid. Anu knew something was wrong because she had not attempted to enter her password since before lunch. When she had, the password allowed her access to the company network. Anu did not take time to deal with the problem when she suspected one. She was racing against the clock to finish her report.

At the end of her workday on Thursday, Anu was pleased to tell her boss that she would complete and deliver her report with the analysis of the Balmstick product the following morning. "No need," replied Anu's boss angrily. "I just found out that our competitors know about

Balmstick and have already talked to the press about some of the customer concerns expressed by your focus group participants!"

An incident investigation determined that an unidentifiable contractor had accessed Anu's report, which was in a nonrestricted file on her computer desktop. Anu was not careful about physical or electronic security, and she did not report any signs of suspicious activity. The investigation concluded that Anu had done nothing to ensure that those with access to the focus group information, including the participants, understood the information's sensitivity or their obligations to protect it. She had not kept her notes in a locked drawer or a password-protected, encrypted electronic file. And perhaps most problematic, Anu was not attuned to any conditions indicating that existing information safeguards were amiss. While a slow computer might not have been a sign of a hacker or other security problem, an unauthorized password attempt, together with papers out of place and a sticky keyboard, were clearly irregular.

Anu should have reported the suspicious incidents immediately. If she had, she may have been advised to stop working on her computer so a systems specialist could investigate the unauthorized access attempts while a security specialist could check the keyboard for fingerprints. Because Anu ignored signs of tampering and thought her Balmstick market research report was more important, she lost the value of her work, and Balm was not able to collect evidence to make a case against the perpetrator.

If Anu's story has a bright spot, it is the hard-earned lesson that protecting information is sometimes as important as creating it. If you witness any suspicious behavior, become aware of an inadequacy in any precautionary force field element, discover a gap in security, or sense an improper information exposure, you may avoid the devastating consequences Anu faced by reporting the potential problem. If you see an opportunity to improve information protection, you should make your suggestions known. The people in your company whose job function is to develop and maintain your company's information protection strategy need your eyes and ears to watch and listen for opportunities to improve it.

The need for collective vigilance was clear during the office remodeling of "Best Pharmaceuticals," when more than twenty-five construction workers were regularly entering and leaving its facilities. The employees whose offices were affected doubled up in cubicles, offices, and conference rooms. Boxes, tools, and construction materials were everywhere. At first, the receptionist insisted that each construction contractor sign in and out, but that soon became impractical. The receptionist was overwhelmed just trying to explain to visitors how to get around the obstructions and find employees' ad hoc locations. Everyone was inconvenienced by the project and distracted by the general chaos that pervaded the building. Because the conference rooms were used as temporary offices, employees held meetings in hallways or in break rooms where strangers frequently passed. The signs outside the building, which read "Caution: Construction" were practically an open invitation for anyone who was interested to enter the premises.

The R&D director assumed his personal computer containing confidential files, and his hard copy documentation for a new drug application, had been misplaced due to the general confusion caused by the construction. After a thorough investigation, Best's security department determined that someone posing as a member of the construction crew had entered the building and stolen the computer and several boxes of files related to the confidential project. While the security department and receptionists were responsible for providing physical security for company facilities, their goal could not be achieved without all employees actively safeguarding their physical environment. A construction project, move, or any physical change challenges even the best security and facilities experts. They count on employees being mindful, and particularly during any physical disorder, to keep confidential materials locked up when they are not in use, to secure their computers, and to avoid having confidential discussions in places where strangers might overhear them.

After the theft, Best's R&D director worked with the corporate security and facilities departments to set up a secure area for his team's work and to keep strangers, including construction workers, out. The arrangement required extra effort, coordination with several corporate departments, and even moving a few times, but the preventative measures' cost and inconvenience may have saved the company millions of dollars of additional lost information. Reporting a suspicious incident helps your company address a potential vulnerability, strengthen its precautionary force field, and avoid future losses.

Keep in mind that information about security weaknesses, including those that present opportunities for improvement, is generally confidential. Only those within your company who are responsible should deal with law enforcement or the news media if such communication becomes necessary.

Praises and Raises

Your information protection efforts can provide significant value to the bottom line of your company. As discussed in chapter 1, protecting privacy and confidentiality is essential and supports your company's ability to achieve its strategic business objectives. With your help and vigilance, information can be transformed into intellectual assets that enhance your company's future. Your contributions to such transformation may be recognized with praises and raises.

After six years at "Bingham Freeze," a traditional frozen foods company, Rey took a job in the packaging department of "Zap Foods," an organic, state-of-the-art frozen foods company. Rey received a memo from his new manager, Julia, requesting that Rey attend training to learn about new equipment, a hermetic packaging sealer Zap had just acquired. The memo included a chart that compared current packaging costs, quality, and yields with anticipated cost savings, improved quality, and yields from the new equipment.

Rey was surprised that the memo was not marked "confidential." At Bingham Freeze, he was taught the importance of recognizing and protecting any potentially sensitive information. His former employer was victim to a trade secret theft and responded by requiring all employees to actively protect any potentially sensitive information. Rey mentioned to Julia that he thought her memo included confidential information and should probably be marked "Zap Confidential." It took courage for Rey, a new employee and a subordinate, to make this suggestion to his boss. But Rey understood that to ask someone if information is sensitive and therefore should be protected is not criticism. Many people forget that the information they work with daily is uniquely valuable to their company, and it will remain so only if it is safeguarded. Asking his co-worker and boss if the information she shared was confidential helped Zap protect its valuable information and competitive advantage. Julia agreed with Rey and thanked him for his feedback.

During his training on the packaging sealer equipment, Rey learned about the sealing times and pressures of the new equipment and how it would be used to reduce Zap's package damage and leakage. He asked the trainer if the information was Zap confidential. She responded by telling all trainees that certain of the information presented about the new equipment was sensitive and should not be shared outside the packaging department. Rey's question allowed the trainer to have a "teachable moment"—it is more likely that the trainees will safeguard the information because they were notified of its confidentiality when the information was disclosed. Also, because Rey asked his question in a setting where all trainees could hear it, he modeled the kind of participation that helps companies keep everyone alert to the importance of protecting information.

Rey soon had a reputation for being knowledgeable about confidentiality. Co-workers followed his lead and reinforced each other being more conscientious about shielding information. After seeing Rey shred the documents and notes that described the old sealing equipment, his work colleagues did the same. Rey's engagement in protecting information helped transform Zap into a corporation with a positively confidential culture.

Rey's leadership paid off. Julia asked Rey to help Zap formalize an information protection strategy suitable to Zap's entrepreneurial culture. And Rey's information protection efforts were recognized in his performance review, which earned him a bonus and a promotion.

You can make a big difference and perhaps earn praise and other rewards for your leadership if you suggest confidential information protection improvements to your manager or to those whose functional responsibility is to oversee information protection. Your company counts on you to get involved and take personal responsibility for protecting information. Doing so will make you a more significant contributor to your company's achievements. You might demonstrate in your performance review how you have been a role model for your company's information protection strategy and describe its benefits to your organization. While it is easy to apply the ten steps to protect information, it is also an accomplishment. You deserve recognition for contributing significantly to your company's success. The gains achieved and losses avoided from a positively confidential ecosystem may be greater than anyone can ever know.

Chapter 10 Spot Quiz
Support Your Company's Information Protection Ecosystem

(The answer key can be found in appendix D)

If you observe a possible violation of your company's information protection policies, which of the following actions should you take?

A. Investigate it on your own to gather further evidence.

B. Tell the offending person to stop doing whatever he is doing or else you will report him.

C. Wait to see if it happens again before acting on it.

D. Contact the appropriate authorities within your company and provide them with the details of what you observed as soon as possible.

Is the following statement true or false?

If you discover a possible confidential information exposure that seems insignificant, it probably is, and you should not report it. You should only report an incident that is obviously a big problem.

Conclusion

I met Tien Shiah only a few minutes before I was to testify in 2007 as an expert witness in *United States of America, Plaintiff, vs. Tien Shiah, Defendant*. My first impression of him was that he was an articulate, good-looking, well-dressed professional man.

Mr. Shiah had been a senior level product manager for Broadcom Corporation, a technology innovator and global leader in semiconductors for wired and wireless communications. After several years there, Mr. Shiah accepted a position at Marvell, a Broadcom competitor.

Testimony indicated that, during Mr. Shiah's exit interview, a Broadcom attorney reminded Mr. Shiah that he was bound by the Confidentiality and Inventions Assignment Agreement, which he had signed when he first joined Broadcom. The attorney reinforced that Mr. Shiah could not use, and was responsible for continuing to protect, Broadcom's confidential information. According to the attorney's testimony, Mr. Shiah asked the attorney which specific information he *could* use, knowing he would be working for a competitor, though he left the competitor unnamed. The Broadcom attorney suggested that Mr. Shiah hire an attorney if he had such questions.

What would you do in Mr. Shiah's situation? Let's assume you used your midlevel manager's salary to support your family. Would you spend your money on attorney's fees to find out exactly what you could and could not use at Marvell? Maybe not. Perhaps instead, you might do what Mr. Shiah did. He made a copy of the files on his laptop, nearly five thousand in total, returned his laptop to Broadcom, and went to work for Marvell.

Several weeks later, Mr. Shiah's life changed. He was charged with a felony under the Economic Espionage Act (EEA). Once they learned that Mr. Shiah was working for Marvell, Broadcom was concerned that Mr. Shiah may have taken their trade secrets. Broadcom had Mr. Shiah's laptop audited and found that all his files had been copied. Broadcom then contacted the FBI, which works with the U.S. Attorney's office to help companies prosecute those suspected of stealing trade secrets.

Marvell, Mr. Shiah's new employer, fired Mr. Shiah after he was indicted. The unemployed and unemployable Mr. Shiah spent his days and nights preparing for and then watching a court proceeding that would determine his fate. He lost months of work, as well as his new, higher-level position at Marvell.

I do not know what Mr. Shiah intended when he copied the files from his laptop. I do know, however, that many people, without the understanding I have attempted to impart in this book, would assume that the information they work with is theirs. They would not think twice about copying the information they used for one job so they could have it available for whatever reason they may need it the future.

When I ended my law practice at a prestigious law firm to found

Pro-Tec Data, I asked the firm's office manager what I should do with my client files. She asked me, "What do you want to do with them?" I was not sure why I might need them, but I also thought that some client materials might be helpful to me in my new business, perhaps as templates for drafting similar documents. I told the office manager that I'd like to take the files with me, and she invited me to take whatever I wanted. That was in 1985, when, like most people, I did not have a personal computer. Though the files I worked with were stored in the law firm's file cabinets, I felt a sense of ownership because I had helped to create them for the firm's clients. Perhaps because of this personal history, I understood what might have motivated Mr. Shiah to make a copy of all his laptop files. Certainly that was easier to do with Mr. Shiah's electronically stored information than it was for me to pack and move a dozen boxes with hard copy files.

If you were indicted on federal criminal charges of economic espionage because you copied files from your laptop before returning it to your former employer, you might consider it all a big mistake because you didn't intend to steal your former employer's trade secrets—you were just being a pack rat. What if the U.S. Attorney for the Central District of California and the FBI said, "Tough luck. You are being charged with a felony"? What if you were Tien Shiah? You might lose more than sleep. The stress might take years off your life.

My role in Mr. Shiah's case was to help the court understand what was required for Broadcom to establish that its information was a trade secret. As discussed in chapter 3, one critical element is that a company must show that it took reasonable measures to protect the information it claims was stolen. If the company did not take reasonable measures, the information taken could not qualify as a trade secret, and an employee such as Tien Shiah would be free to use it.

I reviewed the Code of Conduct that Broadcom had distributed to its employees and the Confidentiality Agreement that Mr. Shiah signed. These materials did not describe, specifically, what information was confidential. There were no additional materials provided to employees for educating or reminding them about their responsibilities for protecting information. I testified that, even if Broadcom had the best physical and electronic security available, the absence of an employee education and awareness program could render such other protections ineffective.

The court concluded in its Findings of Fact and Conclusions of Law:

> Although Broadcom had numerous measures in place, there were deficiencies in the measures taken by Broadcom. There are a number of measures that Broadcom could have, and should have, taken in order to more effectively keep the information secret ... Broadcom should have trained Shiah about what information is confidential and how to handle confidential information ... Broadcom should have provided regular training ... This training should have included methods for ensuring that information remained protected. Furthermore, Broadcom was not clear about which documents should and should not be marked confidential. Shiah was directed to use a template for all PowerPoint presentations containing markings to indicate confidentiality, but there were inconsistencies about which other documents were marked confidential. Broadcom did not have a comprehensive system in place for designating which documents were and which documents were not confidential. A better system could have made it easier for employees to determine which documents were confidential.

Tien Shiah was ultimately found not guilty of criminal corporate espionage. He was allowed to go home to his wife, who sat in the courtroom every day through his tedious trial. Regardless, the U.S.

government will not pay Mr. Shiah for the time he spent preparing for and in trial. There will be no reimbursement for the hundreds of thousands of dollars he paid to hire a criminal defense attorney. But that is the best case for Tien Shiah, a ruined reputation, months of his life lost in anxiety in the trial, no job, and hundreds of thousands of dollars in debt to pay for a trial for which he was acquitted. The worst case? Mr. Shiah could have been convicted of a felony, faced ten years in a federal penitentiary, and have to pay, on top of his legal fees, $250,000 in fines to the U.S. government. Despite the outcome of the criminal suit, or perhaps because of it, Broadcom filed suit against Mr. Shiah in civil court, which cost Mr. Shiah additional time, money for defense lawyers, and his reputation, whatever was left of it.

Broadcom also paid a price. While the FBI handled the investigation and the U.S. Attorney's office prosecuted the case, Broadcom still had to pay tens of thousands of dollars for its outside counsel who monitored the proceedings. There was also significant time and money spent for countless Broadcom employees and contractors who conducted internal investigations, prepared witnesses, and gathered evidence for the prosecution. The expense far exceeded what it would have cost Broadcom to help its employees become familiar with the ten steps discussed in this book.

The biggest toll, though, may be to Broadcom's reputation. At the time of the trial, the company had over two thousand domestic and eight hundred foreign patents and more than six thousand pending patent applications. The litigation sent a message to Broadcom's customers, business partners, and shareholders: The technology and innovation giant did not even bother to train its employees to understand the worth of its trade secrets, which are foundational to its many patents. The company did not protect the value of this intellectual property with a strong precautionary force field.

There is also a cost to you if you are an American taxpayer. As a taxpayer, you paid for the FBI to investigate the case and for the U.S. Attorney to prepare and prosecute it. These costs would likely have been avoided if Broadcom's employees had created a positively confidential ecosystem.

The EEA makes trade secret theft a federal crime for a reason. Trade secret thieves are stealing our country's competitive abilities, and we need our government to prosecute these perpetrators. Your efforts to protect your company's secrets will help stop thieves. If everyone in your organization applies the ten steps described in this book, business processes and technologies can reinforce a clear understanding of what is confidential and how such information should be maintained. A corporate culture will develop where individuals collectively safeguard information and avoid loss. In such a culture, someone like Tien Shiah, who worked hard all his life to become a product manager, would have known that copying thousands of Broadcom files from his laptop before leaving the company could land him in prison and not in a promoted position at Marvell.

Had Mr. Shiah been thoughtless or daring enough to take the information anyway, you could have saved your tax dollars because the U.S. Attorney would have had an open-and-shut case against him. It would have been clear that, despite Broadcom doing all that was reasonable, one bad person had stolen trade secrets.

You can do better than Tien Shiah. By following ten easy steps, you can contribute significant value to your company and avoid situations where you might have to defend yourself against the United States (or any other government), use your life savings to pay your defense attorneys and penalty fees, and then go to prison. With the help of your colleagues, you can create an organizational culture that helps you, your company, and everyone in it, as well as the rest of us taxpayers, save money, time, and reputations. We can all be more productive by using our resources and our innovative potential as a powerful force for good.

Afterword

Positively Confidential in Ten Proven Steps

We have explored ten themes of profound import to your personal career goals and your company's success in the marketplace of products, services, and ideas. In the course of this book, one step at a time, I have articulated why protecting information matters, how to construct a precautionary force field, and what to do when you detect something is amiss that indicates potential information vulnerability. I have discussed practices to identify the information that must be guarded, assert its confidentiality, determine your need to reveal sensitive information, and limit its exposure. We examined appropriate precaution and protection levels and the security technologies and processes that should be utilized to achieve them. I summarized your confidentiality obligations and how you can live up to them.

Looking at the future's accelerating pace of change, it is difficult to know what surprising new challenges await us. Yet we can say with certainty that some current trends, which have helped make intellectual property the gold bullion of the twenty-first century, will intensify: globalization, outsourcing, increasing reliance on computer technology and digital information, and utilization of interactive Web 2.0 and 3.0 technologies, such as wikis, blogs, and social networking tools. As a result, already fierce competition will escalate, and intellectual property will become even more coveted by your adversaries and its protection imperative to your company's viability and success.

Based on more than twenty-five years of experience, as one who helped define, frame and articulate what confidential information protection is and should be, I can assure you that no matter what happens in the future, these ten proven steps to protecting your company's secrets offer necessary, vital and effective tools for the rest of your professional life.

As you accept with full understanding the responsibility to protect your company's confidential information and trade secrets, I offer this review of the ten steps and their takeaways:

1. Know Why Protecting Information Matters

- Keeping information confidential creates value that allows you and your company to reap your work's rewards.
- Your information protection efforts are essential to achieving your organization's strategic objectives.
- Unprotected information can cause very messy and expensive losses.

2. Understand the Risks of Not Protecting Information

- Loose lips (and other forms of information sharing) can sink your company's ship.
- Information scouts are everywhere, eager to take advantage of you.

- You and other well-meaning employees, contractors, vendors, and customers are easy targets if unaware of the risks.

3. Identify the Information You Need to Protect

- Protect all information that
  - your organization defines as confidential
  - others entrust to your organization subject to nondisclosure obligations
  - is private, personally identifiable information subject to privacy laws
- Protect only the information that needs protecting because overprotection can confuse, waste resources, and negate efforts.

4. Make It Clear That Confidential Information Is Indeed Confidential

- Require a nondisclosure agreement (NDA) to create a relationship of trust.
- Indicate information's confidentiality conspicuously.
- Use confidentiality classifications that identify the owner.

5. Determine Your Need to Reveal Before You Share Confidential Information

- Reveal confidential information only if it is within your job responsibility to do so.
- Divulge confidential content based on each recipient's intended use of it, which should benefit your company in all cases.
- Reveal private information only if the owner consents.

6. Limit Confidential Information Exposure

- Create safe zones, where you cannot be overheard by eavesdroppers or seen by unintended onlookers, before sharing confidential information.

- Minimize the confidential information available in unsafe zones.

- Be conscious and conscientious, remembering that everything you say or do may be a clue to your company's secrets.

7. Apply Digital Security Basics

- Protect confidential documents with passwords and encryption, computer networks with firewalls and access controls, and electronic devices with physical security.

- Maintain strong, hard-to-guess passwords.

- Prevent the inflow of unwanted malware with up-to-date anti-virus and anti-spyware software.

8. Construct the Appropriate Precautionary Force Field

- Employ together and use consistently five baseline confidential information protections: NDAs, limited disclosures, confidentiality notices, digital controls, and physical security.

- Strengthen safeguards for more sensitive information and circumstances that create higher than typical loss risks.

- Use informed good judgment and seek guidance from your company's policies, classifications, and information protection experts.

9. Fulfill Confidentiality Obligations to Others

- Protect and use only as you are authorized
  - your organization's confidential information

- information others entrust to your organization subject to nondisclosure obligations
- personally identifiable information that your company collects from individuals

■ Use another company's confidential information only after receiving permission.

10. Support Your Company's Information Protection Ecosystem

■ Activate your sixth sense so you discern when something seems amiss and might cause information loss or compromise; trust your instincts to be curious.

■ Look for opportunities to improve your company's information protection.

■ Report information vulnerabilities.

■ Be an advocate with your colleagues, reminding them that everyone benefits from a positively confidential corporate culture.

Appendix A

Confidential Information Examples

The following are examples of the types of information that many companies consider confidential. As you review this list, consider which information your company may classify as "Company Confidential: Special Handling" (or similar) or "Company Confidential: Private" (or similar). Both classifications, as described in chapter 3, are subsets of information classified as "Company Confidential."

BUSINESS AND STRATEGY	
Business Models	Business Plans
Business Process Reengineering Plans	Internal Reorganization Proposals
New Product Launch Plans	Prospective Acquisitions or Divestitures
Strategic Plans	Workflow Management Data
PRODUCT DEVELOPMENT	
Detailed Design and Functional Specifications	Development Contracts
Engineering Drawings (for example, Critical Parts and Process Drawings)	Engineering Notebooks
New Product Concepts, Details, and Proposals	New Product Investigations

Performance and Feasibility Studies	Product Analysis Results
Product Development Plans and Schedules	Product Direction
Product Problem Analyses and Status	Product Testing Programs
Software Source Code	Technical Breakthroughs
Technical Support Status	Technology Roadmaps
Unannounced Product Availability Dates	Unpublished Test Results
Unpublished Benchmark Data and Results	

PRODUCTION/MANUFACTURING AND OPERATIONS

Assembly Specifications	Capacity Analysis
Distributor Information	Manufacturing Plans and Processes
Operating Results	Production Procedures and Tests
Quality Goals and Improvement Plans	Quality Issues
Raw Material and Component Sources	Shipment Schedules
Supplier and Vendor Lists, Sources, and Contract Terms	Warranty Reports
Yield Data	

FINANCE

General

Balance Sheets and General Ledger	Bookings Reports
Budgets (Operating and Capital)	Cash Accounts
Commercial Invoices	Corporate Investments
Credit Data and References	Expense Reports
Financial Models	Internal Financial Statements
Inventory Reports	Invoices
Order Backlog	Product Profitability Analysis
Profit and Loss Statements	Profit Margins
Profit Sharing	Projections and Forecasts
Revenue by Product	Stock Option Information (Grants, Exercises, and Allocations)
Unannounced Financial Results	Unannounced Material Events (for example, Large Contract Win or Loss)

Sales Indicators

Accounts Receivable Reports	Contract Profits
Customer P.O. and Sales Order Amounts	Royalty Data
Sales Forecasts	Sales Figures by Region or Product

Costs and Pricing

Cost Reduction Plans	Manufacturing Cost Data
Pricing Proposals	Product Pricing Analysis
Raw Material and Component Costs	

Tax

IRS Filings	Tax Audit and Tax Return Work Papers
Tax Planning and Related Financial Analysis	

MARKETING AND SALES

Competitive Analysis	Competitive Intelligence
Customer Agreement Terms	Customer Lists and Profiles
Customer Information Received Under NDA	Customer Satisfaction Survey Results
Marketing Plans and Strategies	Prospect Lists
Strategic Account Plans	Prospect Lists

HUMAN RESOURCES

Applicant Flow Data	Attendance Records
Disciplinary Matters	Drug Testing Results
Employee Compensation, Salaries, and Benefits	Employee Lists
Employee Medical Files	Employment Offers and Contracts
Employee Personnel Files	Headcount Forecasts and Hiring Plans
Identities of Job Applicants	Internal Telephone Directories
Labor Contracts	Layoff/Downgrade Lists
Organization Charts	Payroll Data
Performance and Merit Ratings and Reviews	Separation Agreements
Travel Itineraries	Unannounced Personnel Changes
Workers Compensation Files	

LEGAL, LIABILITY CLAIMS AND LITIGATION

Attorney-Client Communications	Attorney Work Product
Confidentiality Agreements	Non-Routine Legal Opinion
Patent, Trademark, and Copyright Applications	Pending Legal Actions
Settlement Analysis	Software Licenses

SAFETY AND SECURITY ISSUES

Incident Investigation Files	Security Activity Reports
Vulnerability Studies	

INFORMATION TECHNOLOGY

Database Designs	Data Distribution Architectures
Detailed Design Analyses and Specifications	Development Plans and Schedules
Network Architecture, Configuration, and Diagrams	Passwords and PINs
Processing Schedules	Software Requirements and Specifications
Software Development Methods, Techniques, and Processes	Software Source Code
Services Levels	Systems Documentation and Procedures
Systems Performance Data	Technical Support Status

Appendix B

Sample Confidentiality Notices

Sample Standard Confidentiality Notice

A standard confidentiality notice consists of the information classification, such as:

- [Company] Confidential
- [Company] Confidential: Special Handling
- [Company] Confidential: Private

These should appear conspicuously on all confidential material as the minimum confidentiality notification.

Instructional Confidentiality Notices

It is frequently useful to add confidentiality instructions to the standard classification notice. Confidentiality instructions are always an addition to, and not a substitute for, the information classification notice.

The following are sample instructions that can be added, either individually or in combination, to the standard classification marking:

— Copying this document in any medium, in whole or in part, or disclosing its contents to other than the authorized recipient, is strictly prohibited.

— Disclosure and distribution restricted to [specific project group name] only. Distribution outside of this group requires approval from [specific manager].

— Information contained in this file is confidential only until [specific date], when it is approved for publication. Upon publication, it is nonconfidential and may be distributed freely.

— Internal company document. Not for external distribution. Return to originator within [number] days.

— Transmit electronically only if encrypted using a [Company]-approved encryption program.

— All copies must include this confidentiality notification.

— Do not discuss the contents of this file without the originator's permission.

— Do not remove from [Company] premises.

— Subject to protection obligations in the [Company]-approved nondisclosure agreement.

— Shred before disposing.

— Do not dispose of this material. Return to the originator when review is complete or within [number] days.

— Degauss or overwrite before reusing this electronic storage device.

— [Company]'s obligation to protect this material is based on a contract between [Company] and [other company's name]. Serious legal and business consequences will result from failure to protect this material.

Sample Confidentiality Notices for Specific Applications

Confidentiality notices may be tailored to the communications vehicle or medium to which they are attached. The following are examples of three common confidentiality notice applications.

E-mail Confidentiality Notices

The following notice may be used as a footer on confidential e-mails; however, it may be ineffective if the e-mail is sent in unencrypted form over a nonsecure network, such as the Internet. Messages sent in clear text over the Internet may be presumed nonconfidential because of the nonsecure nature of the network used to transmit the message. It may be particularly dangerous to send [Company] Confidential: Special Handling or [Company] Confidential: Private information unencrypted via e-mail.

[COMPANY] CONFIDENTIAL

This e-mail message and any files transmitted with it are for the intended recipient's sole use and may contain confidential, private, or privileged information. Any unauthorized review, use, disclosure, or distribution is prohibited. If you are not the intended recipient, please notify the sender by reply e-mail and destroy all copies of the original message.

Facsimile (Fax) Cover Sheet

CONFIDENTIALITY NOTICE

The following transmittal contains confidential, private, or privileged information intended exclusively for the person named above. Use or disclosure of information transmitted in error is prohibited. Please contact the originator, at the originator's expense, if you have received this fax in error.

Proposals

The following notice can be included in the body of a proposal where the recipient has signed an NDA:

[COMPANY] CONFIDENTIAL

This proposal is confidential and incorporates, by this reference, the terms and conditions of the nondisclosure agreement dated [date], between [Company] and [prospect company's name]. Pursuant to that Agreement, these materials should be shared with only those individuals who may be involved in your company's providing product(s) or service(s) to [Company]. In the event that [Company] does not purchase product(s) or service(s) from your company, you must destroy the proposal within [number of days, not to exceed ninety] days from the date of this letter.

Appendix C

Contacts for Information Protection Help

This page may be used to create a resource list to get help when you need it.

Company Hotline:_____

☐ concerns may be reported anonymously.

	IT Security	Help Desk	Compliance	Legal
E-mail				
Phone				

	Physical Security	Human Resources	Other
E-mail			
Phone			

Web addresses (URLs) to company policies, training, and other references:

Personal computing and mobile devices and their serial numbers:

Software applications and their license numbers:

Appendix D

Spot Quizzes and Answers

Chapter 1: Know Why Protecting Information Matters

Your information protection efforts support which of the following aspirations of your organization?

A. Marketing punch
B. Great reputation
C. Customer confidence
D. Trust
E. All of the above

Correct Answer: E

Is the following statement true or false?
Although protecting intellectual property is not one of your job responsibilities, you should adhere to information protection principles to earn a pat on the back.

Correct Answer: False. Intellectual property protection is one of your job responsibilities, no matter your position in your company.

Chapter 2: Understand the Risks of Not Protecting Information

Which of the following is the most prevalent threat to your company's confidential information?

   A. Hackers breaking into the computer networks and stealing information from servers

   B. Competitive intelligence professionals searching through all available public information looking for your company's secrets

   C. Industrial spies conducting illegal electronic surveillance of your executives' communications

   D. Well-meaning employees exposing confidential information inadvertently

Correct Answer: D

Is the following statement true or false?

Information scouts only target scientists, engineers, and executives, that is, those with direct access to trade secrets and future business plans. Unless you have a job working with highly sensitive information, you are not likely to be targeted.

Correct Answer: False. Information scouts may target anyone with access to confidential company information.

Chapter 3: Identify the Information You Need to Protect

Which of the following statements illustrate a lack of understanding about identifying confidential information?

    A. Not only is personal or private information subject to company-imposed controls, it is also government-regulated at multiple levels, including state, federal, and international.

    B. Within your company, a compilation of individual pieces of information may have a different classification than any particular individual piece of that information.

    C. Information that is considered confidential in one division of your company does not need to be treated as confidential in other divisions.

    D. You must not rely solely on any inventory of classified information. Such inventories may be outdated or incomplete. You must supplement confidential information examples with both your own informed good judgment and the advice of appropriate authorities within your company, especially when evaluating information that is either not included or for which the classification may have changed.

Correct Answer: C

Is the following statement true or false?

All of your company's confidential information is proprietary, but not all of its proprietary information is confidential.

Correct Answer: True. Some proprietary information, for example, information owned by your company and available on its public Web site, is not confidential.

Chapter 4: Make It Clear That Confidential Information Is Indeed Confidential

Based on current best practices, which of the following statements are true?

A. Sales projections, employee lists, and test methods are examples of information that might be classified as "Company Confidential."

B. Business plans, acquisition strategies, and source codes are examples of information that might be classified as "Company Confidential: Special Handling."

C. Records containing an individual's Social Security number, credit card and bank account information, or medical history are examples of information that might be classified as "Company Confidential: Private."

D. All of the above

Correct Answer: D

Is the following statement true or false?

If a piece of information is clearly marked with its appropriate classification, such as Company Confidential, Company Confidential: Special Handling, or Company Confidential: Private, both in hard copy and in all its electronic forms, then you and your company have done everything that is needed to prove that you have taken reasonable measures to protect it.

Correct Answer: False. Reasonable secrecy measures involve more than labeling documents with their classification.

Chapter 5: Determine Your Need to Reveal Before You Share Confidential Information

Which of the following facts do you need to establish in order to evaluate your need to reveal confidential information?

A. You have to know what the nature of the information is; that is, how it has been classified within your company and what controls are supposed to be utilized for its protection.

B. You have to know if you are authorized to provide the information to those who have a need to know it.

C. You need to identify the person independent of his own claim.

D. All of the above

Correct Answer: D

Is the following statement true or false?

Only your company spokesperson has to worry about what he says in public. The press and business analysts will only quote official sources.

Correct Answer: False. The press, business analysts, and others who report and publicize information about a company rely on many sources, not just official spokespeople.

Chapter 6: Limit Confidential Information Exposure

Which of the following may expose information to risk?

    A. A luggage tag

    B. A request for proposal

    C. Your travel itinerary

    D. Your badge at an industry conference

    E. All of the above

Correct Answer: E

Is the following statement true or false?

Limiting confidential information exposure is not part of your job. It's the job of lawyers, IT security specialists, and uniformed guards.

Correct Answer: False. Every employee is responsible for limiting confidential information loss risk.

Chapter 7: Apply Digital Security Basics

Which of the following security technologies best secures the contents of your laptop if it is stolen?

A. Encrypted hard disk

B. Strong password

C. Cable lock

D. Global positioning system

E. Desktop firewall

Correct Answer: A

Is the following statement true or false?

As long as I am not logged on to the Internet from a wireless network, no one can access my laptop via its wireless port.

Correct Answer: False. Information on your laptop may be accessible through its infrared port even when you are not using your laptop.

Chapter 8: Construct the Appropriate Precautionary Force Field

Which of the following activities or technologies strengthens a precautionary force field but is not one of the baseline confidential information protection elements?

A. Securing your work area

B. Encrypting highly confidential materials before communicating them via the Internet

C. Utilizing digital rights management

D. Ensuring the recipient knows the information is confidential

E. All of the above

Correct Answer: C

Is the following statement true or false?

Obtaining a signed NDA from a confidential information recipient is not enough. You must determine that the recipient has a real need to know the information before you share it. You must also remind the recipient that the information is confidential and she is obligated to protect it.

Correct Answer: True. An NDA is only one of many essential precautionary force field elements.

Chapter 9: Fulfill Confidentiality Obligations to Others

Which of the following circumstances could lead to a tarnished reputation, a decline in sales, and criminal prosecution for you or your company?

A. Failing to adequately protect the confidential information and other intellectual property entrusted to your company by its business partners

B. Integrating, adapting, or building upon the intellectual property of other individuals or companies without proper authorization, whether intentionally or inadvertently

C. Keeping detailed customer or employee personal and private information

D. All of the above

Correct Answer: D

Is the following statement true or false?
There is no danger in using a product idea suggested by a contractor in casual conversation.

Correct Answer: False. Without a clear agreement to the contrary, the owner of a submitted idea may sue to prevent or be compensated for the unauthorized use of his idea.

Chapter 10: Support Your Company's Information Protection Ecosystem

If you observe a possible violation of your company's information protection policies, which of the following actions should you take?

    A. Investigate it on your own to gather further evidence.

    B. Tell the offending person to stop doing whatever he is doing or else you will report him.

    C. Wait to see if it happens again before acting on it.

    D. Contact the appropriate authorities within your company and provide them with the details of what you observed as soon as possible.

Correct Answer: D

Is the following statement true or false?

If you discover a possible confidential information exposure that seems insignificant, it probably is, and you should not report it. You should only report an incident that is obviously a big problem.

Correct Answer: False. Even seemingly insignificant incidents may be a clue that a significant information loss problem exists.

INDEX

330   Positively Confidential

About the Author

NAOMI FINE, Esq., president and CEO of Pro-Tec Data, founded the firm in 1985 to help companies manage and protect confidential information, privacy, and intellectual property. Since Pro-Tec Data's inception, Ms. Fine has served as its principal consultant, incorporating legal, digital security, corporate security, human resource, and audit disciplines. Ms. Fine's depth of knowledge comes from working with hundreds of world-class companies to identify sensitive information, assess needs for protecting it, develop tailored information protection strategies, establish policies and procedures, and provide training and tools that secure competitive advantage.

Pro-Tec Data's clients include many Fortune 500 companies, such as 3Com, Apple Computer, Baxter Healthcare Corporation, Bristol-Myers Squibb, Caterpillar, Charles Schwab, Deloitte, Eastman Kodak, International Paper, Intel, Johnson & Johnson, Levi Strauss, MCI, McDonald's, Michelin, Mobil Oil, National Semiconductor, Nortel Networks, PECO Energy, Procter & Gamble, Qualcomm, Ralston Purina, Rockwell International, SC Johnson Wax, Seagate, Sun Microsystems, Symantec, TD Ameritrade, Unocal, Varian, Visa, and Xerox.

Ms. Fine is frequently called upon as a litigation consultant and expert witness in both civil and criminal trade secret lawsuits to help courts determine if reasonable measures have been taken to protect and establish trade secrets.

Ms. Fine has been cited by *Fortune, Business Week, Wall Street Journal, Time, USA Today, New York Times Cybertimes, LA Times,* and *Industry Standard* as a leading expert in her field. KICU-TV featured Ms. Fine in the CEO profile segment of its Silicon Valley Business program.

An authoritative and enthusiastic speaker, Ms. Fine has been featured by many industry associations, including the American Electronics Association, American Society for Industrial Security, Society of Competitive Intelligence Professionals, Information Systems Security Association, Practising Law Institute, Computer Security Institute, EDP Auditors Association, Association of Records Managers and Administrators, High Technology Crime Investigators Association, Trade Secret Law Institute, and Risk and Insurance Managers Conference. Ms. Fine has been a Continuing Legal Education (CLE) accredited speaker for the American Corporate Counsel Association and has served as a guest lecturer for Golden Gate University's Information Security Certificate Program. Ms. Fine holds an inventor's patent in a Proprietary Information Identification, Management, and Protection system.

Prior to founding Pro-Tec Data, Ms. Fine was a business attorney counseling high technology companies on protection, licensing, and other transactions related to intellectual property. Ms. Fine left the practice of law in 1985 to found Pro-Tec Data and assist companies with the practical, logistical, cultural, and organizational aspects of protecting information and intellectual property.

To contact the author, send an e-mail to:
nfine@positivelyconfidential.com

SPREAD THE WORD!

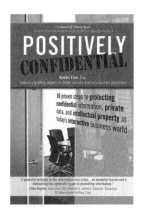

Encouraging every employee in your company, as well as every contractor, customer, supplier, business partner, and other business colleagues to read this book will

- Strengthen your company's information advantages
- Establish your company's intellectual assets
- Save you and your company time and money
- Increase your company's value
- Enhance your reputation and career prospects

To order more copies of this book:

Reasonable Measures Publishing
orders@positivelyconfidential.com
Paperback original: 336 pages
ISBN: 978-0-9800268-0-1

Reasonable Measures Publishing offers bulk order discounts for corporations, institutions, and other organizations.

NOTES